C000090237

MOUNTAIN WALKING IN AFRICA : 1
KENYA

Dedication

For Corinne

'Like wind in the desert...'

MOUNTAIN WALKING IN AFRICA : 1
KENYA

DAVID ELSE

Robertson McCarta

First published in 1991 by

Robertson McCarta Limited
17-18 Angel Gate
City Road
London
EC1V 2PT

© David Else 1990

Managing Editor Folly Marland
Editorial Assistant Ruth Keshishian
Designed by Gail Tandy
Maps by Jill Bitten
Production by Grahame Griffiths
Typeset by The Robertson Group, Llandudno
Printed and bound in Italy by Grafedit SpA. Bergamo.

This book is sold subject to the condition that it shall not, by way of trade
or otherwise be lent, resold, hired out or otherwise circulated without the
publisher's prior consent in any form of binding or cover other than that
in which it is published and without a similar condition including this
condition being imposed on the subsequent purchaser.

British Library Cataloguing in Publication Data
Else, David
    Mountain walking in Kenya. – (Mountain walking in Africa)
    1. Kenya, – visitor's guides
    I. Title
    916.762044

ISBN 1–85365–205–9

Every care has been taken to ensure that all the information in this book
is accurate. The author and publishers cannot accept responsibility for
any loss, injury or inconvenience sustained by readers using this book.

Forthcoming title in this series: **Mountain Walking in Tanzania,
Zimbabwe and Malawi**

Contents

Series Introduction

The Mountains and Highlands of Africa

For most people images of an African landscape typically include wide savannas, impenetrable forests, desert, or tropical coastline. Few would regard the continent as suitable for recreational walking, but the mountains and highland areas of Africa are now becoming recognized as an ideal holiday destination for ramblers, trekkers and backpackers of every standard.

Although the mountains of Africa may not be high by world standards, the major peaks still tower impressively above their surroundings. Kilimanjaro, at more than 5800m/19,000ft the highest mountain in Africa, rises as a huge snow-capped dome over 4300m/14,000ft above the surrounding plains and is visible for many hundreds of kilometres in any direction. Mount Kenya also stands alone, at over 5100m/17,000ft, with its jagged peaks and shining glaciers dominating the surrounding foothills and farmlands.

Yet despite their height and imposing nature, both these mountains are ideal for walkers. Any person of reasonable health and fitness can reach the summit of Kilimanjaro and get to within a few hundred metres of the top of Mount Kenya without specialist equipment or technical ability.

But Africa offers more than just these two giants. Across the eastern, central and southern regions of the continent (that is, south of the Sahara and east of the Zaire basin) hills, plateaux and highland areas offer a wide range of routes for walkers of all interests and standards. Africa can provide anything from gentle bird-watching strolls through light woodland to multi-day backpacking expeditions across a barren landscape of bare rock and ice.

Access is straightforward: this part of Africa is no longer a distant destination reserved for wealthy hunters or eccentric adventurers. Many thousands of visitors are attracted by the Indian Ocean beaches or the thrill of watching animals in the great wildlife areas such as Maasai Mara or the Serengeti. This mass tourism means reasonably priced and readily available air flights, which bring many African capitals within easy reach of Europe or North America.

Then, once in Africa, walkers can easily escape the crowds. It is possible to drive, or travel by public transport, to the highland areas and the start of the approach routes. There is no need for lengthy 'walking-in' hikes, or long treks through foothills involving the support of four-wheel drive vehicles or pack animals. This makes the African mountains ideal for visitors with limited time to spare.

On the mountains and hills of Africa, walkers pass through a fascinating selection of landscapes formed by volcanic action and the colossal forces of a continent splitting apart, or made from ancient rock weathered over millions of years by water, ice or the baking sun. And, as an integral part of this landscape, walkers can witness the trees and other plants that have evolved specially to cope with the unique weather conditions, the prolific wildlife for which Africa is so famous and the fascinating peoples who make the highland areas their home.

Walkers also enjoy the experience of being in remote or seldom-visited regions of a relatively unexplored and unknown continent. The mountains of Africa create a unique impression of isolation or untouched virgin territory. Although this is probably due more to imagination than actual fact, the impression is reinforced by the knowledge that less than a hundred years ago many of Africa's mountains were part of geographers' legend and remained unseen or unclimbed by Europeans.

The series

The books in the *Mountain Walking in Africa* series provide complete and accurate information on routes in the mountains suitable for walking, i.e. rambling, hiking, backpacking or trekking. (For purists there are distinctions between these various terms but the basic concept is the same for each one.) Walking is for everyone; no specialist equipment or technical knowledge is required. No mountaineering or climbing of any sort is included in the books in this series. On some routes a short section of scrambling may be involved, but on the vast majority of walks described you could (if you wanted) safely and confidently keep your hands in your pockets!

Not all the mountains in Africa are included in this series. For a variety of reasons, such as a harsh climate or difficult access, many African mountains and highland areas are not suitable for walking. Similarly, every place where walking is possible cannot be included: most foothill areas are densely populated and extensively farmed, while many of the plains areas are national parks reserved for wildlife where visitors are not allowed to enter on foot. However, in the mountain areas the scenery tends to be more spectacular and the walks themselves far more interesting than in the lowlands or plains.

So while it is theoretically possible to walk anywhere in Africa, this series contains a selection of routes in various mountain and highland regions to provide a wide range of walks of different grades and conditions in a variety of settings. This series therefore contains all the information required by both beginners and experienced walkers, and also by newcomers and those familiar with conditions in Africa.

Readers will find that some of the route descriptions are very detailed, which is helpful for inexperienced walkers or those unfamiliar with African conditions. Even for experienced walkers some routes involve testing conditions or require specific information in order to avoid confusion or ambiguity. In certain areas conditions dictate that a local guide is essential, therefore detailed descriptions are unnecessary and, in the appropriate sections, information on how to hire a guide and a selection of suggested desinations is included instead.

However, many walkers feel that walking, by its very nature, should be a relatively unstructured activity and believe that in-depth route descriptions deny mountain walking much of the spontaneity and fluidity that is usually its very attraction. So, while some route descriptions are very detailed, in other cases this has been deliberately avoided.

Every route description also contains information on recommended approaches (for drivers, hitch-hikers, and those using public transport), recommended times to visit, special conditions, accommodation, campsites, supplies, water, porters, guides, wildlife and people.

Thus the books in this series contain something for everyone; ramblers and trekkers, experts and the inexperienced, newcomers and old Africa hands. We trust there will be something here for you, to help you discover for yourself the freedom, exhilaration, challenge and enjoyment of walking in the mountains of Africa.

Acknowledgements

The author would like to thank the following people, without whom it would not have been possible to write this guidebook.

In Britain: Genevieve West (Trailfinders), Alan Morgan (Africa Travel Centre), Alan Marls, Toby Harrison, Peggy Bitten.

In Kenya: Alan Dixson, Njagi Gakungu, Iain Allen, Ian Howell, Paul Clarke, Malcolm Gascoigne, Idi Lewarani, Major Aussie Walker, Chrissie Aldrich, Jane and Julia Barnley, Mike Wylie and Marie-Lousie Boley, Dave Monk, Ed Sadd, James M'Bugua, John Bisley, David Furnivall, Steve Barnes, Kate Watson, Peter Pickernell, Mo Hussein, plus various members of the Uvambuzi Club, the Mountain Club of Kenya and the Nairobi Hash House Harriers.

The Kenya field research team: Jill Bitten and Nicci Haynes (cartographic research), Robin Saxby (medical officer), Mike Salisbury (equipment consultant), Matt Oglethorpe, Aidan Leheup and Corinne Hunter (additional practical and logistical support).

Contributors: Geoff Mercer, Alex Tyson, Jim Rudolph, Paul Roden, John Siskovic, David Shavell, Mary Rooney, Mike Wood, Charlotte Melville.

Kenya - Introductory details

Official title - The Republic of Kenya.

Capital - Nairobi.

Main airport - Jomo Kenyatta International, 16km from Nairobi.

Independence from Britain - 12 December 1963.

Government - Parliamentary democracy.

Head of State - His Excellency Daniel arap Moi, President and Commander-in-Chief of the Armed Forces.

Position in Africa - Between latitudes 4 degrees N, 4 degrees S, straddling the equator. Bordered to the east by the Indian Ocean and Somalia, to the north by Ethiopia and Sudan, to the west by Uganda, and to the south by Tanzania.

Area - 582,600 square kilometres, 224,900 square miles. (About the size of France.)

Population - 23,000,000 (1988) and expanding rapidly. Main groups of different ethnic origin: Kikuyu; Luo; Maasai; plus numerous other smaller groups. Significant minorities originating from Europe and the Indian sub-continent.

Languages - Numerous indigenous languages and dialects. Kiswahili (often referred to as Swahili) is the common lingua-franca. English is the official language and widely spoken. In very remote rural areas English, or even Kiswahili, may not be used or understood.

Religions - Established Christian faiths (Catholic and Protestant), usually church or mission based, or locally founded Christian sects. Also traditional (anamist) beliefs, Islam (particularly on the coast), Hindu and Sikh minorities.

National Holidays - Easter, Christmas, and New Year's Day. 1 May (Labour), 1 June (Madaraka, Self Government), 10 October (Moi Day), 20 October (Kenyatta), 12 December (Independence). Idd el Fitr is a movable feast celebrated by Muslims at the end of Ramadan falling on 14/15 April (1991), 3/4 April (1992), and approximately 11 days earlier every year.

Time - GMT plus 3 hours.

Voltage - 240 volts.

Newspapers - 3 Kenyan dailies in English. Foreign papers and magazines available in Nairobi.

Unit of currency - Kenya shilling (KSh or /-), divided into 100 cents.

Exchange rates - 1 US dollar = 25/- approx, 1 UK pound = 40/- approx (April 1990).

Banks - Many banks in Nairobi, open weekday mornings until 2 p.m. and some Saturdays until 11 a.m. Money can also be changed in large hotels. Airport banks are usually open 24 hours a day.

Airport departure tax - US$20, payable in hard currency only.

Prices

Prices in the book are quoted in Kenya shillings and were correct at the time of going to print. The date given after each price quoted refers to the time it was correct. When converting to a hard currency, use the rates quoted here. Although the prices in Kenya shillings may increase, the exchange rate changes also, and the eventual cost to the visitor remains generally the same.

Glossary

In Kenya a number of Kiswahili words (or from other African languages) are used as everyday terms by English speakers. Various words from English also have particular or different meanings.

askari - guard
banda - small basic building for accommodation
boma - traditional homestead
centre - small settlement
chai - tea
dam - small artificially created lake or pond
drift - ford
duka - small shop
hoteli - tea shop or small rural eating house
lugga - dry river bed (in the north)
manyatta - traditional homestead and cattle pen (Maasai and Samburu areas)
matatu - small van or bus for carrying passengers
moran - warrior (Maasai or Samburu)
murram road - dirt road
mzee - respectful term for old man (pronounced m'zay)
mzungu - white person
shamba - smallholding or plot of land
safari - literally journey, but usually used to mean holiday
soda - any bottled fizzy drink
watu - people (i.e. local people)

On mountain route descriptions the following terms are used:

bluff - cliffs or outcrop
cairn - pile of stones for waymarking
caldera - correct term for a crater caused by subsidence of a volcanic cone
col - low point in ridge or between hills
corrie - short, steep-sided, bowl-like valley (created by glaciers)
outcrop - exposed rocks
scree - loose stones
tarn - small lake

Abbreviations used:

SK - Survey of Kenya (maps)
M - thousand (referring to map scales)
4WD - four-wheel drive (vehicles)
pp - per person
ppd - per person per day
ppn - per person per night
d - double (room)
s - single
bb - bed and breakfast
hb - half board
fb - full board
b - banda
c - camping

All hotel prices quoted are per person or per double per night, unless otherwise stated.

Key to maps

════════	tarred road	Δ		summit
═══───	graded road	⅄⌢⌢		cliff
═ ═ ═ ═	ungraded road	Ɛȝ		boulder
_ ⁔ ⁀ _	path	) (		col, bridge
··········	undefined way			glacier
⊢⊢⊢⊢	railway	△		campsite
─·──	park boundary	▢		building
···─··─	national boundary	○		town
⌇⌇⌇	river	●		gate

Part One
PRACTICAL INFORMATION

Introduction

Since the earliest days of explorers and white hunters, Kenya's visitors have gone 'on safari' to see the fascinating wildlife on the wide grasslands of the African savanna. In more recent times, the sandy beaches and guaranteed sun of the Kenyan coast have become another tempting attraction, so that now Kenya receives over half a million visitors every year.

Mount Kenya, Africa's second highest mountain, is also a popular destination, where any reasonably healthy person can get to within a few hundred metres of the summit without technical knowledge or specialist equipment.

Mountain Walking in Kenya shows that this country offers more than just one big mountain, however, by describing a selection of walking routes of various lengths and degrees of difficulty in hills, mountains and highland regions all over Kenya.

Some of the routes described in this book involve at least two or three days' walking through high altitude forest or open moorland, which usually means camping or staying in huts. Other routes are much shorter, through rolling grassland or pleasant hill-country, and are more suitable for one-day hikes and rambles. Also, it is often feasible to cover one section of a larger route as a day-walk while, in certain cases, a number of different day-walks from the same base are possible. For reassurance, or to lighten the load, guides and porters can be hired and, in some cases, are highly recommended.

If the wildlife and beaches are an added attraction, Kenya's reliable communications and established infra-structure make it easy to combine mountain walking with these other aspects, even for visitors with limited time. Details about specialist tour operators or agencies able to make the necessary arrangements are included. For visitors unused to African conditions, an organized mountain trek provides an ideal introduction before setting out alone.

This book also contains advice about the clothing and equipment required for mountain walking in Kenya and detailed information about weather conditions, transport and accommodation.

All that is required from you, the visitor, is an adventurous spirit and a desire to discover for yourself the unique world of the mountains of Kenya.

Travelling to Kenya

In the grand old days of travel visitors to Kenya usually arrived by ship at the port of Mombasa, before journeying 'up country' to Nairobi or the game parks by train. A few intrepid adventurers, however, did make the long journey from Europe by land, crossing half the continent of Africa - mainly on dirt roads and sometimes on no roads at all - through Egypt, Sudan and Uganda.

Today, as air travel becomes increasingly affordable, most visitors to Kenya fly direct to Nairobi, but for those with unlimited time it is still possible to travel overland from Europe, either independently or with an organized tour. This journey usually involves crossing the Sahara Desert and the dense forests of the Zaire river basin, but is generally reckoned to be one of the great long-distance overland routes in Africa, or even the world.

Flying direct

Although flights to Nairobi can be bought in any major city in the world the widest choices, and some of the cheapest fares, are available in London. Various airlines offer flights from London to Nairobi including Aeroflot, Air France, Air Sudan, Egypt Air, Ethiopian Airways, Gulf Air, KLM, Lufthansa, Olympic Airways, PanAm, Sabena, Saudia and Swissair, but these all involve at least one change of aeroplane. British Airways and Kenya Airways both have daily direct London - Nairobi flights which do not involve changing planes.

From the USA several airlines offer New York to Nairobi fares but these usually involve changing plane in Europe. Visitors with time available may find it cheaper to fly to London and buy the ticket to Nairobi there. Some specialist agencies can arrange both parts of the flight. Alternatively, the second section of the flight can be arranged in advance through an agency in London.

When buying a flight to Kenya it is recommended that you contact a specialist travel agent who can advise on the various choices available and find a flight that suits your requirements. Prices charged by the airlines and the travel agents vary considerably but often reflect the reliability of arrival and departure times, the quality of the service and the frequency of the flights. The price may also depend on the length of time you plan to stay in Kenya and whether you want a fixed-date or open-ended return.

Other points to check when buying a ticket is the day of the week on which the flight leaves and its scheduled arrival time in Nairobi. Unless you have pre-booked your first night's accommodation, the best time to arrive in Nairobi is in the morning.

Some recommended travel agents in London are listed overleaf.

Africa Travel Centre (4 Medway Court, Leigh St, London WC1, Tel 071 387 1211) cater particularly for independent travellers and specialize in flights and overland expeditions to and around Africa, and also offer an interesting selection of adventure holidays and self-drive tours.

Trailfinders (42-48 Earls Court Rd, Tel 071 938 3366, and Kensington High St, London W8, Tel 071 938 3939) arrange flights and overland tours to many destinations in Africa and also provide vaccinations, insurance and a travellers' reference library.

STA Travel, with several offices around the UK and an Africa Desk at their London branch (117 Euston Rd, London NW1, Tel 071 388 2266), provide cheap flights and tours for students and independent travellers, and can also arrange travel insurance.

Wexas International (45 Brompton Rd, Knightsbridge, London SW3 1DE, Tel 071 589 3315) is a membership club providing a wide range of discounted international flights and tours, plus various other services such as insurance and an information service.

Travelling overland

Independent travel

For overland travellers the Nile Route to Kenya, through Egypt and Sudan, has been closed since the 1983 outbreak of civil war in southern Sudan. So overlanders still intending to visit Egypt must fly from Cairo to Nairobi. The political situation in Sudan means conditions are likely to remain difficult for overland travellers.

The second option, the Trans-Sahara Route, is longer than the Nile Route but (at the time of writing) less prone to political problems which may affect overland travellers. This route starts in Algeria and passes through Niger, Chad or Nigeria, Cameroon, Zaire and Tanzania before reaching Kenya.

Many travellers drive their own vehicle, while others take public transport or hitch-hike. Whichever way you travel remember that overland routes through Africa are long and arduous. Travellers with vehicles should have at least some mechanical knowledge and prepare their vehicles for very rough roads and tracks, as well as irregular and unreliable fuel supplies. Those relying on public transport or hitch-hiking should be prepared for long waits, crowded vehicles and frequent breakdowns.

To prepare for an overland journey to Kenya read a good manual or guidebook (see the Books section on p57). For information about specially designed overland vehicles and advice about driving in Africa contact Overland Ltd (Link Road, West Wilts Trading Estate, Westbury, Wiltshire, BA13 4JB, UK, Tel 0373 858272).

Organized tours and expeditions

If the intrepid style of independent travel does not appeal, but you still would like to reach Kenya by land, various companies organize overland tours between London and Nairobi which provide an interesting and inexpensive way of getting to Kenya. Taking an organized tour of this nature removes many of the logistical problems encountered by independent travellers while still being fairly adventurous. By the time you arrive in Nairobi many aspects of life in Africa will be familiar, and you can be more confident about travelling alone around Kenya to and from the mountain regions.

Some of the larger overland companies also operate tours and safaris around Kenya or to other countries in the region such as Zaire, Tanzania, Malawi and Zimbabwe. These can usually be booked directly at the company's office, or through a specialist travel agent such as those previously mentioned (see p14). You may decide to travel overland one way and fly back from Kenya, so an agency able to arrange both aspects of your journey has obvious advantages.

Many overland companies advertise their tours in the travel sections of national newspapers or in specialist travel and outdoor magazines. These include: Exodus Expeditions (9 Weir Rd, London SW12 0LT, Tel 081 673 0859); Kumuka Africa (42 Westbourne Grove, London W2 5SH, Tel: 071 221 2348); Tracks Africa (12 Abingdon Rd, London W8 6AF, Tel 071 937 3028). Contact these companies direct for brochures, price lists and further information.

HABIB'S CARS LTD.

The Camper People of Kenya

One of the oldest and most experienced Car Hire firms in Kenya specializing in 4WD Vehicles and Camping Cars

Awarded the International Award of Tourism (GOLDEN HELM)

AGIP HOUSE HAILE SELASSIE AVENUE
P.O. BOX 48095 NAIROBI KENYA TELEX: 23257 AL–SHARIFF
TELEPHONE: 20463, 23816 & 20985 FAX NO. 339357

The go-anywhere self drive SUZUKI CAMPER

All Campers fully equipped with kitchen utensils, gas cookers, lamps, jerry cans, blankets, pillows, mattresses, etc.

The Climate of Kenya

Kenya can be divided into four geophysical regions, each with its own distinct climate pattern: the Rift Valley and Central Highlands enjoy temperate conditions in the Rift rising to near-arctic conditions on the mountain peaks of the Highlands; Western Kenya is at a lower altitude and so warmer and wetter than the Rift or Highland regions; the coast is also hot and wet but cooled by sea breezes; and the north is generally desert or semi-desert plain with high temperatures and low rainfall. Most of the mountains covered in this book fall in the Rift Valley, Central Highland and northern regions.

Seasons

Kenya has two rainy seasons; 'the long rains' from March to May and 'the short rains' from mid-October to mid-December. In the west and on the coast the rainy seasons can be longer, while they tend to be shorter in the north. Rainfall also tends to be higher in the mountain or highland regions. Usually, during these rainy seasons, the mornings are dry but become increasingly humid until the rain falls in the afternoon or early evening.

The two dry periods are June to October and mid-December to February. Visitors who come for the beaches or for the game-viewing prefer these times as the weather is less inclement and animals in the national parks easier to spot, so these have become Kenya's 'high' tourist seasons.

Visitors who come to walk on Kenya's main mountains (e.g. Mount Kenya, the Aberdare Range and Mount Elgon) are also usually restricted to the dry seasons. At these times the trails are easier to follow and less water-logged, and the lack of rain allows longer periods for walking between huts or campsites. The less frequently visited mountain areas that are covered in this book (e.g. The Cheranganis, the Lenkiyio/Mathews Range, and the highlands around Maralal) are all farther to the north where the seasons follow slightly different patterns. Walkers visiting these remoter parts of Kenya can arrive in Nairobi during the 'low' season to avoid the crowds and take advantage of cheaper rates for hotels, rented cars and organized tours. If you intend to walk on some of the higher mountains as soon as the rains have eased, spending some time in the lower ranges will help you become acclimatized. During this early part of the dry season water supplies are more reliable, although some of the less frequented trails might be overgrown and harder to follow. (The weather pattern on each mountain is covered in greater detail in the relevant chapters.)

Temperatures

On the mountains of Kenya the minimum and maximum daily temperatures vary only slightly throughout the year. During a single day, however, the temperature range is wide and is affected very largely by the altitude. Generally, the temperatures likely to be encountered on the mountains described in this book are as follows:

In sunlight, on the lower slopes at around 2500m/8,000ft temperatures can be a comfortably warm 68°F/20°C, and a pleasant 60°F/16°C at around 3500m/11,500ft. However, even on the lower slopes, temperatures drop rapidly at sunset (between 6 and 7 p.m. all year) and nights can be cold (around 40°F/4°C). At the highest altitudes, above 4000m/13,000ft, temperatures during the day in direct sunlight are usually around 50°F/10°C, but are always below freezing point (32°F/0°C) when the sun is obscured. On the main peaks of Mount Kenya (all over 4500m) night temperatures are always below freezing and often drop to 8°F/-10°C or even lower.

Wind is another important factor to consider. On the lower slopes a cooling breeze is often very welcome but on the higher mountains strong winds can make the already low temperatures seem even colder.

On the high mountains (e.g. Mount Kenya and Mount Elgon) mornings tend to be clear as the cloud level is usually below 2500m/8,000ft. As the temperature increases during the morning, the cloud level also rises and by midday the peaks are usually covered. Cloud continues to build up and rain (or sleet and snow in cold conditions) is likely to fall in the afternoon or early evening. During the later evening and night, as the temperature falls, the cloud returns to its lower level.

On the highlands around Maralal daytime temperatures are usually warm, around 70°F/21°C, and suitable for walking at all times, although early starts are recommended. Nights are misty and surprisingly cold (sometimes dropping to 35°F/2°C). On the Lenkiyio/Mathews Range temperatures are warmer so the cool mornings and warm evenings are the most pleasant time for walking in these hills. During the afternoons temperatures can rise to around 85°F/30°C. Walking is reasonably pleasant when passing through open shady forest, but on some of the lower trails that climb steeply through dense bush conditions can be uncomfortable. Nights can be cold, sometimes dropping to around 40°F/4°C.

(Regional temperature conditions that differ from the general outlines above are covered in more detail in the relevant sections.)

MOMBASA
Best value on The Island!

Opened in the 1920s, we've moved with the times. Every room has a telephone, radio, TV and video, and most have air conditioning.

The Manor Hotel

THE COAST'S FAVOURITE RENDEZVOUS

NYERERE AVENUE, P.O. BOX 84851, MOMBASA
TELEPHONE: 314643
TELEGRAMS: MANORIAL MOMBASA
FAX: (254-11) 311952

TWO GOOD HOTELS FOR TRAVELLERS IN KENYA

NAIROBI
Best value in Town!
(2kms city centre)

Set in 5 acres of beautiful gardens, our accommodation is in the best tradition of a country hotel, yet equipped with telephones, TV & video.

FAIRVIEW HOTEL

THE COUNTRY HOTEL IN TOWN

BISHOPS ROAD, P.O. BOX 40842, NAIROBI
TELEPHONE: 723211, 722878, 27444
TELEGRAMS: FAIRVIEW NAIROBI
TELEX: 25584 FAIRVIEW
FAX: (254-2) 721320

In Kenya

Accommodation

In Nairobi

Before you get to the mountains, it will probably be necessary to spend a few days in Nairobi to change money, confirm a homeward flight, send postcards, or buy food supplies and last-minute items of equipment. Apart from these practicalities, staying in Nairobi for a short while is recommended: you will meet other tourists or walkers, who may be able to offer advice or encouragement; you can familiarize yourself with Kenyan ways (some visitors unused to conditions in developing countries occasionally experience 'culture-shock') and maybe even learn a few words of Kiswahili. You will also have a chance to get used to the increase in altitude. The importance of acclimatization cannot be over-emphasized, and will be covered in greater detail later in this book. Remember that Nairobi itself is at 1500m/5000ft and you may feel lethargic for a few days until you get used to the altitude. Don't try to do too much too soon. The lure of the mountains will be strong and you may be tempted to escape from Nairobi's crowded city streets as soon as possible, but to head straight for the hills may make things harder and possibly even dangerous later on.

Nairobi has a wide range of hotels catering for all tastes and budgets. City centre hotels include The Nairobi Hilton, a full international standard hotel with all facilities (d 3000/- or US$140, 1990), the Sixeighty Hotel, a mid-range hotel with most facilities (d 1100/- or US$65, 1989), and The Iqbal, a clean and safe budget hotel popular with young travellers (d 150/-, 1990). Hotels outside the city centre include The Panafric, a mid-range hotel with most facilities (d 1800/- 1990), and Mrs Roache's Guest House, with dormitories and a campsite which is often full of overland travellers and their vehicles (50/- bed, 40/- camping ppn, 1990). Also outside the city centre, but near enough for visitors to walk into town, is the Fairview Hotel. This is a very popular hotel, set in quiet grounds, with most facilities and a selection of rooms of varying standards and rates, and an ideal place to stay before starting a tour or safari, or to rest for a few days after a mountain walking expedition (d 620/- to 900/- bb, 1990). Nairobi also has a Youth Hostel and a YMCA and YWCA which both take visitors.

For complete details about hotel accommodation in Nairobi use one of the many general guidebooks about Kenya. (For full details see the Books section on p57.) The official Kenya Tourist Offices in many countries around the world can also provide information about accommodation in Nairobi and other main centres.

Outside Nairobi

Outside Nairobi, the choice of hotels is often limited. A few larger towns do have mid-range hotels, but generally accommodation is restricted to a local style 'boarding and lodging' house (often called a B & L), usually attached to a restaurant or bar. These hotels are often very rudimentary (some even double as brothels), but they provide all the basics at a very reasonable price. I have stayed in countless B & Ls all over Kenya and always received good service and never experienced any difficulties more serious than power cuts (carry a torch), bed-bugs (use a sleeping-bag), or loud music from the bar downstairs (take ear-plugs, or go down and join in the fun!).

Note that local snack bars or tea shops are often called 'hotels', or *hotelis*, but do not offer accommodation.

In some towns camping is possible in the grounds of a large hotel, or at a nearby farm, guest-house or country club. Unofficial camping in towns is not recommended. In villages and country areas, ask permission from the chief or local police officer before pitching your tent. For more details about campsites in Nairobi, in other towns, or in rural areas see *The Camping Guide to Kenya* by David Else (details on p58).

On the mountains

In the mountain areas themselves, standards and types of accommodation are very varied. On Mount Kenya's popular routes huts have been built, while on the less frequented mountains facilities are non-existent and walkers must be fully self-contained. Information about accommodation, either on the mountain or at the beginning of the walk, is included in each route description.

For the routes on Mount Kenya a tent is not necessary as walkers can stay in huts but, for anything longer than a day's walking on most of the

Two Tarn Hut, on Mount Kenya's Summit Circuit Route

other mountains covered in this book, a full set of camping equipment is highly recommended. A tent provides shelter from the elements and gives you complete freedom and flexibility. On the less frequented mountains an almost unlimited number of idyllic spots exist which are ideal for camping. Even on the popular routes a tent allows you to pitch near the huts, and take advantage of their facilities, without having to reserve space or predict an exact arrival date. Alternatively a tent means you can avoid these sites altogether and enjoy the beauties of the mountain in isolated peace. For full details about the tents and camping equipment recommended for walkers in Kenya see the Equipment section on p40.

Food and supplies

In Nairobi, international style menus are available at good hotels and restaurants, while less elaborate, but no less filling, meals can be bought at a number of reasonably priced restaurants around the city centre that cater for tourists and locals. In the back streets, just outside the city centre, and around the markets and stations are cafeterias and snack bars serving simple but tasty local food at very low prices.

Outside Nairobi basic eating houses can be found in all but the smallest towns. Typical menus include some kind of meat, chicken, bean or vegetable stew served with rice or maize meal. Fish, eggs and plantain bananas are sometimes available. Kenya's links with the Indian sub-continent means samosas and chapatis can often be found. Traditional African menus usually make few allowances for vegetarians (even vegetable stews are often cooked in a meat stock), but most large towns have at least one Asian restaurant serving vegetarian food. For more details about places to eat and the types of food available refer to one of the general guidebooks mentioned in the Books section on p57.

For food supplies to carry on your mountain walking trips Nairobi is fairly well stocked. The following items should satisfy most appetites, and are readily available from numerous food shops and supermarkets in Nairobi: lentils, noodles, pasta and rice and various kinds of dried vegetables; tins of fish, tomatoes, beans and spaghetti in tomato sauce; cheese, sausages, bacon, packets of cooked meat, tins of corned beef; bread, crackers and porridge oats; dried soups, tea, instant coffee, drinking chocolate, Ovaltine, dried milk, sugar; tins of margarine, jam, honey and peanut butter; biscuits, nuts, dried fruit, chocolate. (Be prepared for occasional shortages of essential items such as sugar or flour.) The City Market on Muindi Mbingu St has an excellent selection of fruit and vegetables.

Outside Nairobi and other large towns food supplies are often limited. When preparing for a mountain walking trip, for reliability, all food except fresh fruit and vegetables should be bought in Nairobi. The specially designed, freeze-dried, high-energy, quick-cooking mountain food found in Europe or America is not available anywhere in Kenya.

Remember that uncooked meats are unsuitable for long expeditions unless they can be kept in refrigerated conditions, and that water boils at a lower temperature at high altitudes which means rice, lentils and dried vegetables take longer to cook. I have found fresh vegetables more suitable for mountain walking in Kenya; they are cheap, readily available, nutritious, stay usable for at least a week, cook quickly (when chopped small), and create little or no waste disposal problems. They are no heavier than tinned food and require much less fuel to cook than dried items. Fine pasta, such as vermicelli, can be bought in Nairobi and is perfect for high altitudes; it is light to carry, very quick to cook and goes well with anything.

If your Western palate still craves for more, all kinds of imported specialities are available at the shops in Westlands Shopping Centre or the nearby Sarit Centre just off Wyaki Way on the north-west side of the city. The chocolate bars in Africa have familiar brand names and, although they are more oily (to withstand higher temperatures) than their Western namesakes, they are no less welcome and energy boosting when you're hungry at 4000 metres!

Transport

To get from Nairobi to the various mountain regions visitors should either hire a car or use public transport. In some areas hitch-hiking is also possible. This book describes road transport only, which is generally more convenient than internal flights or the train for all but the longest journeys.

Car hire

A number of companies in Nairobi rent saloon cars or four-wheel drive (4WD) vehicles, suitable for off-road conditions. Cars can be hired by the day with an additional charge made for the distance covered, or for the week with an unlimited distance allowance. A visitor's national driving licence is generally sufficient (without endorsements), but an international driving licence (available from any national motoring organization) is more readily accepted. An additional charge is made for insurance and a deposit is usually required although this can normally be paid with a credit card. A collision damage waiver (CDW) is generally available at a small extra cost and highly recommended as it exempts you from a large proportion of costs incurred in an accident caused by a third party. Check all these details carefully before hiring a car. Rates and standards vary considerably and a number of unreliable companies do try to take advantage of unwary tourists. The following companies in Nairobi can be recommended:

Concorde Car Hire (Agip Service Station, Wyaki Way, Westlands, P.O. Box 25053, Tel 743008/011); Hertz (corner of Kaunda and Muindi Mbingu Streets, P.O. Box 42196, Tel 331973/4, 727493); Let's Go Travel (Caxton House, Standard St (near the British High Commission), P.O. Box 60342,

SELF DRIVE CAMPING SAFARIS

A different approach to camping

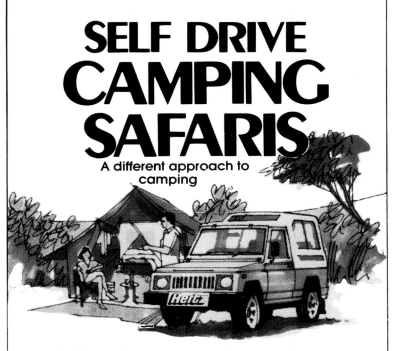

Self Drive Camping means total freedom of movement. Hertz offer rugged go-anywhere four-wheel drive vehicles for the more remote areas or comfortable estate cars for the nearby reserves.

Each self-drive camping vehicle comes with tentage and all the necessary camping gear.

For further details contact

Hertz

Nairobi, Muindi Mbingu Street, Box 42196 Tel: 331960

Mombasa, Moi Avenue, Box 84782 Tel: 316333/4

Malindi, Harambee Road, Box 365 Tel: 20069

Tel 29539/40, 340331); Payless Car Hire (Koinange Street, P.O. Box 49713, Tel 338400); Suntrek Tours and Travel (Monrovia St, P.O. Box 48146, Tel 335741, 334965, 25679). For camper vans and specially adapted 4WD vehicles with roof-mounted tents, as well as conventional vehicles, contact Habib's Car Hire (Agip Service Station, Haile Selassie Ave, P.O. Box 48995, Tel 20463, 23816, 20985).

The most popular 4WD hire-car is a small Suzuki (often called a 'jeep'), available in 2- and 4-seater versions. Expect to pay 450/- to 600/- per day, plus 5/- to 8/- per kilometre, and 200/- to 300/- for CDW (1990 prices). Petrol costs around 11/- per litre and a Suzuki does around 10km to the litre. The standard of driving in Kenya is not good and road accidents are common. Be prepared for other vehicles behaving unpredictably and watch out at all times for people and livestock on the road.

Public transport
For walkers without a vehicle Kenya has a good, if fairly erratic, public transport network. Buses and shared taxis usually cover long-distance routes between major towns. Shared taxis are invariably large Peugeots (generally referred to as 'Peugeot taxis') which tend to be fast and comfortable, while buses tend to be the opposite, although on busy routes between main towns luxury express coaches are also available. *Matatus*

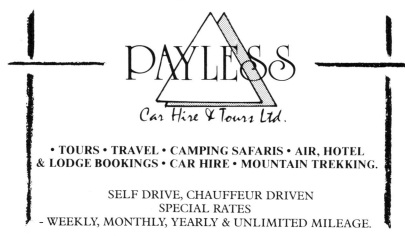

PAYLESS
Car Hire & Tours Ltd.

• **TOURS** • **TRAVEL** • **CAMPING SAFARIS** • **AIR, HOTEL**
& LODGE BOOKINGS • **CAR HIRE** • **MOUNTAIN TREKKING.**

SELF DRIVE, CHAUFFEUR DRIVEN
SPECIAL RATES
- WEEKLY, MONTHLY, YEARLY & UNLIMITED MILEAGE.

DAIHATSU • LANCER • MAZDA • MINI-BUSES • NISSAN • TROOPER 4WD
• PAJERO 4WD • PEUGEOT • PICK UPS • SUZUKI • TOYOTA •

OLYMPIC HOUSE, KOINANGE STREET
P.O. Box 49713 • Tel: 338400 • Fax: 339779 • Telex: 23130
NAIROBI • KENYA.

We Live Up To Our Name

(minibuses) supplement the bus services either around cities and towns or between the towns and their surrounding rural centres. On routes through well-populated areas, matatus tend to run more often than buses and are often very crowded. In remote or sparsely populated regions bus and matatu services are less frequent.

Costs are hard to generalize but, as a rule of thumb, expect to pay about 1/- for every two or three kilometres covered in a long-distance bus and about double that for Peugeot taxis. Around town, buses and matatus charge 3/- minimum. Out to the suburbs will cost between 5/- and 10/- (1990). Taxis around Nairobi will charge at least 70/- for a short ride across the city centre, 100/- for rides to the suburbs, and 250/- from the city centre to the airport. Arrange the fare before getting in a taxi.

Car vs public transport
A car makes reaching most mountains straightforward, but means you always have to return to the vehicle at the end of your walking. Some walkers find it restricting and unsatisfying to backtrack in this way. Another problem involves leaving the vehicle unattended in areas where this may not be safe. To avoid this a local person could be hired as an *askari* (guard). Alternatively, have a non-walker in your party willing to drop off and collect the walkers at the beginning and end of the route. Safe parking places, where they exist, are included in the individual route descriptions.

Concorde
CAR HIRE

THE KEY TO CAR HIRE
**For a wide range of vehicles
self-driven or chauffeur-driven with superb service and reliability**

P.O. Box 25053 Nairobi, Telephone 743008/743011
Telex 22366 "BRENT X"

25

Although walkers using public transport may find it harder to reach the mountains, there are advantages in being without a car. It will not be necessary to find somewhere safe to leave the vehicle and the mountain can be ascended and descended by different routes which avoids backtracking.

For every route covered in this book, the general approaches, by car and public transport, are fully described.

Hitch-hiking

In many African countries the distinction between public transport and hitch-hiking is blurred. Bus services may be infrequent or non-existent so local lorries will carry passengers for a small payment. In Kenya, however, it is often possible to hitch in the manner more usually understood in Europe or North America. People with saloon cars (Kenyan residents or visitors) will often stop, and even some truck drivers will give you a lift without charging. If a charge is made it is usually the same as the bus fare, but if you are unsure check with the driver before getting in.

In remote areas of Kenya where public, and private, transport is harder to find you might get a lift with an official police or government vehicle. Once again, check if payment is expected.

Walkers without a car may find themselves sometimes using a combination of public transport and hitch-hiking to reach the mountains.

Yare Safaris Co. Ltd.

TRACK GORILLAS –
VISIT SERENGETI

TANZANIA
Ngorongoro - Serengeti - Lake Manyara - Mt. Kilimanjaro - 7 days.
EGYPT - ZIMBABWE - BOTSWANA - RWANDA

Yare Safaris also operates - **KENYA**
Fortnightly departures to **TURKANA** - 8 days
Fortnightly departures to **MAASAI MARA & RIFT VALLEY**
Weekly **Camel Safaris** - 7 days.   **Mt. Kenya** - 7 days.
Indian Ocean Beach Cottages - by the day.

BOX 63006 NAIROBI, KENYA.
TELEPHONE: 559313   TELEX: 23044

Remember that the traditional hitch-hiking thumb sign might be regarded as a rude gesture so, unless you can see that the driver is a European and unlikely to misinterpret your signal, use an outstretched hand, pointing along the road, in the same manner as the local people.

Organized walking tours.

If this is your first time mountain walking in Africa, you may regard the prospect of hiking in such an exotic location as more than a little daunting. Even if you are an experienced walker, or are already familiar with conditions in Africa, you might want to enjoy your hiking without the concern of route-finding or unencumbered by the weight of a large rucksack.

In either case you could consider joining an organized walking tour. A number of companies, based in Kenya and in other countries, arrange a variety of tours, often called 'walking safaris'. (*Safari* literally means 'journey' in Swahili.)

When visiting remote regions, the local knowledge of a guide and the support of porters or pack animals are often essential to a successful walking tour. If time is limited an organized walking safari can reduce such logistical concerns, although for many walkers, preparing for the journey or expedition is all part of the enjoyment.

Photographic Safari in Kenya

Exclusive luxury tented safaris off the beaten track, for families and small groups

Safari with Cheli & Peacock

Kenya: Cheli & Peacock Ltd. P.O. Box 39806, Nairobi, Kenya. Tel: Off. 749654/5/6. Telex: 22388, TRIHO, Fax: 254-2-740721

U.S.A.: Sues Safaris Inc. P.O. Box 2171 Ranchos, Palos Verdes, Ca 90274 Tel: (800) 541-2011/California (213) 541-2011

England: Twickers World, 22 Church St. Twickenham, TW1 3NW, U.K. Tel: 01-892-8164/7606. Telex: 25780. Fax: 01-892-8061

Even on the more straightforward routes some visitors find that organized tours provide a useful introduction to African mountain conditions. You may prefer to join an organized safari first, to get the feel of things, before setting out on your own. This way you will be more prepared mentally and physically, and be aware of your own capabilities and limitations.

Walking safaris operated by reputable companies are led by experienced and informative guides, giving you the opportunity to learn more about the landscape and environment you pass through and about the birds and animals you might encounter along the way. Some companies also offer hikes and treks through less strenuous lowland regions, or through national parks and reserves where unaccompanied walkers are not usually allowed.

If you are a photo buff, or just a keen amateur photographer looking for that elusive wildlife close-up, walking safaris allow you to experience something of the old hunting spirit, stalking animals in their natural habitat, in the protective company of experienced guides and rangers but armed yourself with nothing more than a zoom lens.

The following tour companies organize walking tours, or safaris that include walks as part of their itinerary, in Kenya.

Explore Worldwide run a camping safari for small groups that visits Lake Nakuru, Maasai Mara and other major game-viewing areas of Kenya, and also includes bush walking in the remote Loita Hills region (16 days, £1050 pp, 1990). An extension to this tour, at Mombasa and Lamu, is also available. Explore also have tours in Zaire, Tanzania, Malawi, Zimbabwe and many other African countries, many of which include walking and trekking. Clients who want to visit several parts of Africa can link two or more tours. (1 Frederick St, Aldershot, Hants GU11 1LQ, UK, Tel 0252 344161, Fax 343170, or Adventure Centre, 1311 63rd St, Suite 200, Emeryville, CA 94608, USA, Tel (415) 654 1879, Fax 654 4200.)

Exodus Expeditions organize walking tours on many East African mountains including Mount Kenya and the Aberdare Range in Kenya (17 days, £1790 pp, 1990), Kilimanjaro in Tanzania, plus others in Malawi, Uganda, Zimbabwe and Botswana. The tours aim to escape the usual tourist routes and are planned to allow time for acclimatization. (9 Weir Rd, London SW12 0LT, Tel 081 675 5550.)

Sherpa Expeditions offer two tours on Mount Kenya: one combined with a vehicle-based safari to the lakes and northern deserts of Kenya (23 days, £1640, 1990); the other with trekking on Kilimanjaro, plus an extra week's game-viewing safari. (131a Heston Rd, Hounslow, Middlesex TW5 0RD, Tel 081 577 2717.)

Executive Wilderness Programmes specialize in custom-designed walking tours on the mountains of East Africa including Mount Kenya and many of the smaller, more remote, mountain ranges. Clients can choose their own destination and, to a certain extent, their own level of service depending on budget. Technical mountaineering routes plus game

TROPICAL ICE

East Africa's original adventure safari company, specializes in discovering new trails through unspoiled wildernesses, where you will only see game animals and nomadic people. We also lead expeditions up Mount Kenya, through scenery you'd never have imagined existed. If your idea of an African Safari is something a little more stylish and adventurous than the average package tour, contact us:

Iain Allan, Tropical Ice Ltd, PO Box 57341, Nairobi, Kenya
Telephone:740811, Fax:740826

safaris and coast extensions are also available on request. (32 Seamill Park Crescent, Worthing BN11 2PN, Tel 0903 37565.)

A selection of recommended Nairobi-based companies is listed here, roughly in order of cost, to indicate the range of safaris available.

Cheli and Peacock organize exclusive tented safaris with regular departures from Nairobi. Guided walks are arranged each day in the area around the camp according to clients' wishes and ability (US$520 ppd for two clients, US$297 ppd for eight on the 'custom classic' safari, US$713 ppd for 2, US$391 ppd for 8 on the 'original', 1990). Also available are specially designed safaris, to suit the needs of individuals, families and small groups, visiting areas of the clients' choice including national parks in the fertile savanna, the northern semi-desert region, or the high mountain areas. (US$620 ppd for 2, US$340 for 8, 1990.) (PO Box 39806, Nairobi, Tel 749654/5/6, Fax 740721.)

Of the specialized walking safari companies Tropical Ice stands out as one of the best for quality and experience. They organize high-level walking tours on Mount Kenya, along little-used paths away from the usual tourist routes, and lower-level treks through hills in a remote part of Maasailand. Walks can also be tailored to suit clients' specific requirements or include technical mountaineering. (Scheduled departure safaris US$170 ppd for 6.) (PO Box 57341, Nairobi, Tel 740811, Fax 740826.)

Kentracks is a specialist walking safari operator offering treks in areas of particular scenic and cultural interest, varying in length from half-day

AFRICA TRAVEL CENTRE
01-387 1211
Compact Group Safaris
KENYA, TANZANIA, BOTSWANA, EGYPT, NAMIBIA, ZIMBABWE
Personalised Luxury Safaris
TO ALL AFRICAN COUNTRIES
Overland Budget Safaris and expeditions
LOW COST AIR FARES
To all African countries ■ Car Rentals Hotels and Visas.
BROCHURES ■ ADVICE ■ INFORMATION
AFRICA TRAVEL CENTRE LTD.
4 Medway Ct, Leigh St, London WC1H 9QX.
RUSSELL SQUARE ⊖ KINGS CROSS
The Friendly Way To Africa

excursions around the Ngong Hills to 15-day safaris, combining treks on Mount Kenya and some of the remote northern peaks with game-viewing in the national reserves. (C/o Bruce Safaris, Kenwood House, Kimathi St, PO Box 47964, Nairobi, Tel 27311, 339094, Fax 331756.)

Bushbuck Adventures operate a selection of scheduled departure mid-range camping safaris including walking tours, ornithological tours, game-viewing tours and a camel trek. Safaris can also be tailored to suit clients' wishes and include walks on Mount Kenya, the Aberdare Range or in any of the other mountain areas of Kenya. (Gifillan House, Kenyatta Ave, PO Box 67449, Nairobi, Tel 60437 729639, 212 975/6/7, Fax 728737, after hours 521554 or 26 Newnham Green, Maldon, Essex CM9 6HZ, UK, Tel 0621 853172.)

Yare Safaris operate a wide range of tours, many of which start from their hostel and campsite in Maralal, some 300km to the north of Nairobi. Clients taking their walking safari (600/- ppd, 1990) are accompanied by local Samburu *morans* (warriors). Also available are camel safaris through the semi-desert plains of Samburuland and along the banks of the Ewaso Ngiro River; clients can ride the camels or walk during the day, and in the evening guided walks from the camp are arranged. Yare are also the only company running overland safaris to visit the mountain gorillas of Zaire. (Yare Safaris Adventure Travel Centre, 1st floor, Union Towers, Corner Moi Ave/Mama Ngina St, PO Box 63006, Nairobi, Tel 725610, 725618.)

Gametrackers specialize in low cost adventure trips and offer walking

DISCOVER KENYA with

Monrovia Street
P.O. Box 48146, Nairobi, Kenya.
Telephone: 335741/334965/25679
Telex: 25621 TREK KE
Fax: 334965

SUNTREK
TOURS & TRAVEL LTD

Personalised attention and care in:-

- Car Hire — (Weekly/Monthly rates available on request)
- Hotel & Lodge reservations
- Local & International Airline Bookings
- Exclusive "Tailor made" Safaris
- Camping Safaris
- Transfers from Rail and Airport

tours in the Aberdare Range, as well as safaris by canoe, camel and mountain bike. Other safaris include game-viewing in the main national reserves and rugged truck safaris to Lake Turkana and the northern deserts. (Ground Floor, Finance House, Banda St, between Koinange and Loita Streets, PO Box 62042, Nairobi, Tel 338927, 22703, Fax 330903.)

Reservations for safaris, especially with the companies catering for mid- and low-range budgets, can often be made 'on the spot' at very short notice. For the high-range companies bookings should usually be made in advance, but on trips with scheduled departures space may be available at late notice. Contact the companies direct for more information.

Specialized treks on Mount Kenya, for beginners or experts, are also arranged by Naro Moru River Lodge and Mountain Rock (Bantu) Lodge, both positioned at the foot of Mount Kenya. For complete details about their hotel accommodation, campsites, tours and mountain huts see the Mount Kenya section on p75.

Most visitors who come to Kenya to walk in the mountains also like to see some other aspects of the country, its wildlife and human inhabitants. Several of the companies already mentioned also run vehicle-based safaris, visiting national parks and reserves to view the animals, or travelling to the remoter northern districts to experience the harsh landscape and see the fascinating local peoples. Other Nairobi-based companies operating non-walking safaris, include: Special Camping Safaris, Gilfillan House, Kenyatta Ave, PO Box 51512, Nairobi, Tel 338325,

EXPLORE

Wildlife & Natural History Adventures

With Explore you can view big game in Kenya, track mountain gorillas in Zaire, experience exotic wildlife in the Okayango Delta and Kalahari. You could join our Zambezi River Safari, or see the unique wildlife of the Galapagos and Amazon rainforest. Other adventures tackle Malawi, Tanzania, Namibia, Madagascar, Nepal, Sri Lanka, Sumatra, Borneo, Papua New Guinea, Brazil and Patagonia. Small groups, expertly led.

Over 90 tours, treks, safaris and expeditions in 50 countries around the world. 2-4 weeks. Regular slide shows in Central London. For big colour brochure contact: **Explore Worldwide (RMG), 1 Frederick St, Aldershot, Hants GU11 1LQ. ☎ 0252 344161** (24hrs).

WALKING IN E. AFRICA

Fully supported treks throughout east and southern Africa, from Kenya, Uganda and Tanzania to Malawi, Zambia and Zimbabwe. Whether your goal is a tough climb of Mt Kenya or Kilimanjaro, a cultural journey through Masai or Samburu homelands or wildlife viewing on foot with experienced guides, Exodus has the right trip for you.

Our free full colour brochure is packed with exciting opportunities for those with the spirit of adventure. Have you got your copy yet?

Exodus Expeditions (dept TK), 9 Weir Road, London SW12 0LT, Great Britain.   Fax: 081-673 0779   Telex: 8951700
081-675 5550 (days)   081-673 0859 (24 hrs)

...TRAVEL WITH THE EXPERTS!

Nairobi Office:
Great Expectations Ltd.
P.O. Box 10788
Nairobi
Kenya
Tel: (254 2) 26770
Canadian Representative
Barbara Sutherland
5408 - 99th Street
Edmontoni
Alberta, Canada
Tel: (403) 441 9042

European Representatives
Kimbla Mantana
7 Oak Street
Lechlade Glo
Gl7 3AX
Great Britain
Fax: 036753438

Mr Rene Martig
1997 Havte -Nendas
Switzerland.
Fax: 27/88 31 33

TRAIL BLAZING IN KENYA
The first of its kind, Trail Blazing in Kenya allows you the experience of a life time to see the countryside and meet the people like no other safari can. Highlights include:

- **Spining your wheels** Throughout the back roads of Kenya. - Supping with the chief and elders of Mihuti village. - gazing into the lost world within the volcanic wall of Mt. Longonot.. - hiking to the historical site of the Mau Mau caves in Mt. Kenya. - ...and more!

Kenya spectacular Safari- A thrilling 22 day luxury safari and beach holiday, visiting the Aberdares, Mt. Kenya, Samburu, Nakuru, Lamu and Mombasa.

Kenya Adventure - A unique camping safari that brings the excitement and fascination of the African bush alive - 14 exhilarating days camping in Samburu, Masai Mara and Amboseli Game Reserves plus a visit to Mihuti Village as guests of a local Kikuyu tribe.

20072 (budget camping safaris to Maasai Mara, 10-day truck trips to Lake Turkana); Safari Seekers, Jubilee Insurance Exchange, Kaunda St, PO Box 9165, Nairobi, Tel 26206, 334585 (budget camping safaris from three to seven days to Amboseli, Maasai Mara, Tsavo and the lakes, mountain bike safaris in Hell's Gate and Lake Bogoria National Parks); Therion Safaris, Data Centre Building, 3rd floor, Kenyatta Ave, PO Box 70559, Nairobi, Tel 24998, 20317 (budget camping safaris around Kenya and into neighbouring countries, tailor made safaris for groups, camping and cottage lets on the coast.) Great Expectations, 1st Floor, Protection House, corner Parliament Rd/Haile Selassie Ave, PO Box 10788, Nairobi, Tel 26770, Fax 26584 (lodge safaris to Maasai Mara and Amboseli, 6-day safari circuit of Maasai Mara, Lake Naivasha, Samburu National Park including a night at Treetops, camping and mountain bike safaris.)

If you plan to take more than one safari, or intend to visit several different areas within Kenya, it may be easier to arrange everything through a travel agent. The specialist agent arranging your flight to Kenya will be able to make some bookings for you but, if you want your itinerary to be flexible, the finer details should be arranged in Nairobi. A good travel agent can make all your bookings with safari or trekking companies, reserve rooms at hotels in Nairobi or lodges 'up country', provide a rental car and make all your internal travel arrangements, including local flights and trains to the coast. Nairobi has many travel agents, some of which are disreputable, but the following companies can

S A F A R I   A D V E N T U R E

We offer Biking, Walking and Canoeing safaris to many destinations like: Turkana, Maasai Mara, Ewaso Ngiro River, Chalbi Desert, Marsabit, Amboseli, Aberdares, and the Rift Valley Lakes, using our special safari vehicles.

Contact us for full information

Gametrackers (K) Ltd.
P.O. Box 62042, Nairobi, Kenya.
Finance House, corner of Banda/Loita Streets.
Telephone: 338927/22703
Telex: 22258 TRACKER, Fax: 330903

Gametrackers (K) Ltd.

Bisley Advertising Ltd.

Let's Go

For
- All Air Travel
- Tours and Safaris
- Car Hire
- Bookings at over 200 Lodges and Hotels in Kenya.

Years Let's Go Travel

TOWN OFFICE: Caxton House, Standard Street,
P.O. Box 60342 Nairobi, Kenya. Tel. 29539, 29540, 340331.
BRANCHES: Karen Above Karen Provision Store, Tel. 882742
Muthaiga Muthaiga Shopping Centre, Suite No. 10, Tel. 750034/36.

be recommended:

Let's Go Travel (Caxton House, Standard Street, PO Box 60342, Tel 29539/40, 340331, Fax 336890) offer an efficient booking service, popular with tourists and residents, and represent a wide range of companies with walking and general safaris to suit all budgets and time limits. Let's Go are a particularly useful agency for walkers in Kenya as several of the mountain lodges, plus isolated hotels and campsites in the remote mountain areas covered in this book, are also represented.

Suntrek Tours and Travel (Monrovia Street, PO Box 48146, Tel 335741, 334965, 25679, Fax 740524) can provide rental cars, including chauffeur driven services and airport transfers, make hotel and lodge reservations, and arrange local and international airline bookings.

Smart Tours and Travel Ltd, Jubilee Insurance Exchange, PO Box 42830, Nairobi, Tel 25850, 332671.

Safari Travel, K.C.S. House, Mama Ngina St, (near the Hilton), PO Box 31120, Nairobi, Tel 22290/1, Fax 334944.

With the advent of fax machines it is now possible for visitors to contact a travel agent from their home country to make all the necessary travel and tour arrangements before their arrival.

For more information about tour companies, safaris, accommodation inside and outside Nairobi, shops, restaurants, events and tourist news, a selection of free tourist booklets is available from hotels and travel agents in Nairobi. These include *What's On*, *Tourist's Kenya*, and *Tourist Index*.

Mountain Club of Kenya (MCK)

This club consists of Kenyan citizens and ex-patriates working in Nairobi and caters for climbers, mountaineers and hill walkers. The MCK meets every Tuesday evening (from 8 p.m.) in their clubhouse at Wilson Airport. Groups of members within the club usually organize walks and expeditions and may be able to include visitors, although car space is usually limited. Many visitors regard the MCK as an unofficial tour company or information service but you should not expect unlimited advice or help with transport or accommodation from members. Secondhand clothing and gear is often advertised for sale on the club's notice board, and visitors looking for walking companions might find other like-minded tourists at the club, or arrange to meet them through messages on the board. The MCK can be contacted by writing to PO Box 45741, Nairobi, or telephoning 501747 (evenings).

Preparing for the Trip

Paperwork

Visas and documents

All visitors to Kenya require a full passport. A temporary passport will not be accepted, even if you only intend a short stay in Kenya. This is also the case if you are travelling overland to Kenya, or planning an extra trip into a neighbouring country such as Tanzania or Uganda. Although passports can be renewed in embassies abroad, it is advisable to have a passport that will remain valid for the entire duration of your trip.

A visa (permission to enter a country, usually in the form of a stamp in your passport, for which a fee is payable) is required for most visitors to Kenya, except for citizens of the United Kingdom and Ireland, West Germany, Spain and the Netherlands who are issued a visitors pass. This is also a stamp in your passport (issued in a straightforward manner, for no charge, at your point of entry) which is valid for one, two or three months but usually renewable.

Visas can be obtained from a Kenyan embassy, consulate or high commission either in your own country if you are flying direct, or in a neighbouring country if you are travelling overland. Visas cannot be issued at your point of entry (i.e. the airport or a border post).

When applying for a visa, or when entering Kenya, you may be asked to show 'sufficient funds' to prove that you can support yourself during your stay. This seems to be an objective appraisal made by immigration officials to prevent 'undesirable' visitors entering the country. At the Kenyan High Commission in London a sufficient amount was deemed to be £250 (1990). If you are in any doubt about the regulations governing visas and visitors passes, and because the regulations themselves can be changed, further details can be obtained direct from your nearest Kenyan embassy or high commission, or from a Kenyan state tourist office.

Immunisations

You may also be required to show certificates proving that you have been vaccinated against yellow fever and cholera. These vaccinations are available from your doctor or a health centre. Also recommended are innoculations against tetanus, typhoid, meningitis and hepatitis A, and a malaria prophylaxis. (No innoculation is available at present; a course of tablets is required.) See your doctor at least eight weeks before you plan to leave to arrange your innoculations. Ensure your doctor is well informed about current recommendations. Alternatively contact a specialist medical information centre.

In the UK, the Medical Advisory Service for Travellers Overseas (MASTA) and British Airways jointly operate a number of travel clinics which can provide authoritative advice and information about immunisations, anti-malaria pills and all aspects of health while travelling. The majority of clinics are open daily and you can normally be seen at very short notice. There are fifteen British Airways Travel Clinics in Britain. For more information and the address of your nearest clinic telephone 071 831 5333.

Insurance
Unfortunately, immunisations cannot protect you from every danger in Kenya, and accidents, although unlikely, have to be prepared for. A good insurance policy is highly recommended. It should cover any doctor's fees or hospital costs incurred while on holiday, and also cover the expenses if you have to be flown home in an emergency. Most insurance policies also cover you against personal liability, cancellation, and loss of luggage or equipment. A number of different policies designed for independent travellers are available and premiums vary considerably. Policies are available from Trailfinders, STA, and the Africa Travel Centre (addresses in Travelling to Kenya section on p13) and several other organizations. Your travel agent may be able to advise. Some policies regard trekking above a certain altitude as potentially dangerous and require an extra premium to be paid. Read the policies carefully and decide which one best suits your requirements.

Money
Prices in this book are generally quoted in Kenyan shillings (see Introductory details on p9). Although Kenya's economy is relatively stable, prices do increase every year. However, as exchange rates also increase at a similar pace, costs to the visitor are likely to remain little changed.

Kenya is used to receiving tourists from many countries and most major currencies can be exchanged for Kenyan shillings without difficulty. US dollars, UK pounds (sterling), French francs, Swiss and German marks are the most convenient.

Travellers cheques are secure as they can be replaced if lost or stolen, but they can be difficult to change outside large towns. Internationally recognized brands are easier to change than cheques from small or obscure banks. Some cash is useful if you need to change money in a place where travellers cheques may not be convenient. In this case US dollars are the most easily recognized and readily accepted.

On entering Kenya you will be issued with a currency declaration form (CDF). Every time you change money keep your receipt and ensure the cashier stamps your CDF. This will be scrutinised by customs officials when you leave the country and also allows you to change surplus Kenyan shillings back into hard currency.

It is usual to barter for trinkets and curios on Kenya's many roadside souvenir stalls, but most other items in shops and markets have a fixed price. Although some unscrupulous traders will try to take advantage, you are unlikely to be overcharged. If you are uncertain about the correct

price for anything ask before buying or check what other shops are charging.
A black market for hard currency does exist in Kenya. In certain places it is possible to get a few shillings more than the official bank rate. Changing money in this way is not recommended as it deprives this developing country of much needed foreign exchange and, more importantly, is strictly illegal.
Small change is always useful for shopping in markets, matatu rides and tips, but is in constant short supply, especially in remote regions. It can be very frustrating when you want a drink at a remote tea shop and the owner cannot provide change for anything larger than a 20/- note!

Budgeting for the trip
So many variables are involved in a visit to Kenya that it is impossible to outline here any average costs. When planning your trip, though, the following aspects should be taken into account. (Prices as at March 1990.)
   Transport. Costs for rental cars and public transport are outlined in the Transport section on p22.
   Accommodation. A selection of hotel prices is given in the Accommodation section on p19. Take into account the number of nights you plan to spend in hotels or B & Ls and the number of nights camping. Official campsites cost around 30/- ppn (1990).
   Food. For supplies when walking allow 100/- to 300/- ppd depending on your menu. Restaurant prices vary also; good quality restaurants charge prices that are generally on a par with their European equivalents, while cheap meals taken in basic local snack bars cost as little as 20/-.
   Miscellaneous. If you intend taking an organized safari during your stay this will add to your costs (details in the Organized walking tours section on p27). If you are planning your own itinerary take into account guide and porters fees where necessary, and include park fees where applicable. (Details in the section on National parks on p73.)
   Extras. This might include: beer (11/- to 30/- per large bottle, depending where you buy); soft drinks (5/-); cigarettes (13/- to 20/- for 20 1990 prices);

Physical and mental preparation

While the mountain walks described in this book do not require any specialist knowledge or experience, you can enjoy your walking to the full if you are reasonably fit and healthy. Remember that walking and carrying a rucksack at altitude is significantly more tiring than in the lowlands. If you do not usually do much recreational walking, it would be a good idea to build up your strength a little before you leave home. If you come out to Kenya completely unprepared physically, this will not only make your walking harder and less enjoyable, but it could also have more serious and even dangerous consequences.
   Mental preparation is also important. Before you arrive in Kenya read

a good general guidebook (details in the Books section on p57). For something lighter try a few novels set in Kenya or the accounts of the early explorers. Keep abreast of recent events by reading newspapers. Consequently when you arrive in Kenya for the first time you will have something of a 'feel' for the place and be more prepared for the mountains and everything else the country has to offer.

Equipment

The equipment required for walking in Kenya is not dissimiliar to that required for mountain walking anywhere else in the world. However, it is important to know about specific Kenyan conditions so that your gear can be planned accordingly. Lightweight walking and backpacking equipment is difficult to find and very expensive in Kenya, so bring all you need with you. Check that any new equipment you buy for the trip will be suitable and that gear you already have is in good condition.

If you are new to mountain walking or general travel in Kenya, and need detailed information, seek expert advice from a reputable outdoor equipment shop and read a good introductory guide or manual (details in the Books section on p57). The following information and advice about clothing and equipment suitable for mountain walking in Kenya will provide a useful introduction.

KARRIMOR RUCSACS, CYCLE BAGS, CLOTHING, SLEEPING BAGS, KARRIMATS AND KS-B BOOTS ARE WORLD RENOWNED FOR THEIR TECHNICAL EXCELLENCE, QUALITY, AND COMFORT.

Since 1958 Karrimor has supplied equipment to many leading international expeditions, including many successful ascents of Everest, and the First Winter K2 Expedition. Karrimor products are now available in over 20 countries worldwide.

EQUIPMENT *for* ADVENTURE

KARRIMOR INTERNATIONAL LTD., PETRE ROAD, CLAYTON-LE-MOORS, ACCRINGTON, LANCASHIRE. BB5 5JP

Footwear

A bewildering range of boots is available made in a wide variety of weights, patterns and materials. The main choices are: light or heavy; leather or synthetic.

Heavy mountain boots, either the traditional leather design or the more modern solid plastic style, are only needed for exceptionally rough terrain or for walking on snow and ice when crampons need to be fitted. Walks of this nature are not covered in this book.

To reduce weight and save energy many walkers prefer to use a pair of lightweight boots. Several different styles are available from specialist manufacturers made either from leather or synthetic material. While not providing the same protection as heavy boots, light boots do provide ankle and sole support and, by being more flexible, they are less likely to chafe and cause blisters. Light boots are sufficient for the conditions likely to be encountered on routes described in this book.

Attitudes towards mountain footwear have changed in recent times and, as walkers have become used to boots of an increasingly lightweight nature, many now find a pair of good quality training shoes (running shoes) to be perfectly adequate. These shoes should be of a strong construction and have a firm sole with good grip. Baseball boots or gym-shoes have thin soles and are not suitable.

Several types of walking shoes are also available, made from leather or synthetic materials, and either based on training shoe design or on a more traditional brogue style. An advantage of their weight and size means walking shoes can be more easily carried in your rucksack when you are not using them, and can also be worn more appropriately around towns or when travelling to and from the mountains.

Bear in mind, however, that shoes of any type do not offer the same ankle protection available from boots, and on the more remote mountain trails a sprained ankle can be a considerable problem. Remember, also, that in mountain conditions training shoes tend to wear out quicker than specially designed walking shoes or boots.

Whichever type of footwear you use for mountain walking in Kenya, comfort is always the most important factor to consider, so any new shoes or boots should be thoroughly tested and broken in before you depart for Kenya. If you already have a comfortable and reliable pair of boots these will be fine.

While walking in Kenya you may be caught out in an afternoon downpour or find yourself tramping through wet grass after heavy dew. Wet feet soon become cold and wet socks can rub and cause blisters, so measures should be taken to protect against this.

Light synthetic boots tend to be less water-resistant than their leather counterparts, but even the best leather is not completely waterproof. Some recent leather boot designs incorporate a special tanning process which prevents water saturation (e.g. Berghaus's Hydrostop 12). This increases water resistance and breathability and allows wet boots to dry more quickly.

Boots and shoes can be waterproofed with a variety of sprays and waxes available from outdoor equipment shops, but generally this process is never completely effective. More important, shoes treated in this way can, in hot weather, make your feet sweat more than usual as the treatment tends to hinder airflow and evaporation. (Note that new leather boots will not readily absorb proofing agents.)

Feet can be more effectively protected by proofing the lower area of the shoe, around the seam fixing the sole, and covering the upper with gaiters. In cold or muddy conditions, gaiters covering ankles and the lower leg also provide an extra layer of insulation or protection, while in dry weather they can be removed allowing shoes (and feet) to breathe adequately. When walking over loose scree gaiters help to keep small stones out of your boots.

A recent development of interest to walkers are socks made from Goretex (a breathable waterproof fabric).

To keep feet dry and comfortable in all weathers carry plenty of spare socks and change them throughout the day as conditions dictate. Socks should be made from natural materials (wool or cotton) and washed frequently. Washing can be dried on the back of your rucksack as you walk.

Traditionally walkers wear two pairs of socks; a thin pair inside a thicker pair seems to be the best combination, but only if there is room inside your boots. Blisters can be caused as much by the boot being too tight-fitting as by being too loose. Remember also that many people have feet of slightly different sizes, so take this into account when finding your own most comfortable combination.

Clothing

For mountain walking in Kenya clothes should be practical, comfortable and versatile. Practical clothes should be suitable for all conditions likely to be encountered: keeping you cool in hot conditions; warm in cold conditions; and dry in the rain. If you sweat or burn, you will lose body moisture, and suffer from dehydration. If you do not keep warm, you use up energy quickly, and soon become tired or ill. If you get wet, you will soon become cold, especially when you stop. Comfortable clothes should be flexible and adjustable; tight-fitting garments restrict movement and cause discomfort. Several thin or medium layers of clothing are more versatile and adaptable than a few thick or heavy items. A layer system based on the following suggestions allows you to make the most effective use of your clothes.

Inner, or base, layer. You will perspire during your walk and the clothing next to your skin absorbs this wetness which becomes cold and uncomfortable when you stop. 'Thermal' vests made of polypropylene are light to wear and do not absorb water. Instead they transmit, or 'wick', the moisture particles away from your skin either into the next layer of clothing or to be evaporated in the air. Thermal vests and undertrousers are available in various styles. Popular makes include Sub 4 and Helly Hanson's Lifa range. As an alternative, Buffalo Clothing's Pertex windshirt and Pertex and pile mountain shirt also provide warmth and insulation without absorbing moisture. If you prefer not to wear synthetic fabrics next to the body a string vest made of wool or cotton does not absorb perspired moisture or keep it next to the skin. Silk vests are light and also recommended for insulation.

Middle, or core, layer. Trousers, shirts and sweaters can be as traditional or as high-tech as your budget and personal preference allows. Cotton or poly-cotton trousers (not jeans), a T-shirt, a woollen shirt plus a sweatshirt and pullover will be fine for conditions found on most of the mountains described in this book, although you can save weight and bulk by using clothing specially designed and manufactured for outdoor activities. Various synthetic fabrics (e.g. Airlight, Polapelt, Ultrafleece) are employed to make items of clothing that are cool yet tough for hot weather or warm yet light for colder conditions.

For the higher mountains a windproof jacket should be added to this middle layer. The most suitable type has a zipped opening, high collar, an integral hood and close fitting elasticated cuffs and waist. Various makes of jacket are available which combine padded and closely woven fabrics to make a warm and windproof layer.

The outer, or shell, layer. When conditions get very cold or wet, clothing should be totally windproof and waterproof. Once again, you can choose between traditional or modern designs and materials. Waxed cotton coats are warm and waterproof but heavy to carry. More suitable is a nylon anorak, or cagoule, with a hood. Overtrousers provide vital protection and insulation. If you are exerting yourself, condensation is trapped inside the shell layer, which makes your other clothes wet. To avoid this, various cagoules are available made from a fabric with a special membrane which is waterproof yet breathable (e.g. Goretex, Sympatex). Lined and quilted versions are also available adding an extra layer of warmth to your clothing system for cold conditions. Good quality clothing of this type can appear expensive but, if these garments are used

Travelling Light in Kenya?

Travelling Light makes an exclusive range of smart but practical cotton clothing for men and women travelling in hot countries.

We also supply high quality accessories like insect repellents, money belts, sunglasses, flight bags and rucksacks.
Same day despatch of in-stock orders world-wide.

Write or ring for **free** colour catalogue to

TRAVELLING LIGHT (MWK)
Morland House, Morland, Penrith, Cumbria CA10 3AZ
Telephone 09314 488

properly, they can be very effective and make your walking far more enjoyable. A wide range of clothing designed specially for climbers, mountaineers and mountain walkers is produced by Karrimor. Their products are available from good outdoor equipment suppliers.

After continued use the effectiveness of Goretex, and similar materials, is often impaired by the residue left by evaporated perspiration. This problem can be solved by rinsing the inside of the garment in warm water.

A completely different approach to the problems of designing clothing suitable for a wide range of conditions has been taken by Buffalo Clothing (Meersbrook Works, Sheffield 8, UK, Tel 0742 588481). Their unique 'Double-P' system, pile and Pertex, is used to make a range of mountain clothes and sleeping bags which rely on the quick drying, warmth-retaining properties of the fabrics. Because there has been no attempt to make these products completely waterproof they are comfortable, practical, versatile and reasonably priced.

Other items of clothing useful when walking in the mountains are a warm hat or balaclava, gloves, and a scarf or neck-tie. A bush hat that keeps off sun and rain, and a warm hat or balaclava for cold conditions, are recommended. Sunglasses (or snow goggles for the snow-capped peaks) cut out glare and help you avoid headaches.

In very cold conditions use the other clothes you will be carrying to add more layers. An extra T-shirt or sweatshirt and a pair of tracksuit trousers worn between the bottom and middle layers will increase the insulation level.

In Africa, military style clothing is practical but best avoided. Almost every African country has its memories of at least one civil war, rebellion or coup. In remote regions you may be mistaken for a soldier or mercenary. If you find army trousers suitable dye them blue or sew on some different coloured patches.

When reading through this section on clothing, the weather conditions on Kenya's mountains may appear too severe for enjoyable walking. This is not the case. With a little planning to allow for seasonal and regional variations, you will enjoy fine walking through Kenya's impressive and beautiful mountain scenery. However, like any mountains in the world, the mountains of Kenya do have their occasional unpredictable periods of bad weather. It is foolish to be unaware of this and not to plan your clothing and equipment accordingly.

After several years' travelling and mountain walking all over Africa, I have found the following set of clothes suitable for walking for most occasions. It is important to keep weight as low as possible. This can be done by carrying the bare minimum of spare items of clothing. Non-specialist items like T-shirts, socks and underwear can easily be replaced in Nairobi.

I wear or carry: one pair of walking shoes, one pair of sandals, four pairs of socks, two pairs of lightweight trousers, one pair of shorts, one thermal vest, three pairs of underpants, two T-shirts, two long-sleeved polycotton shirts, one 'polarfleece' sweatshirt, one light wool pullover, one insulated windproof and waterproof jacket, one nylon cagoule and pair of overtrousers, one pair of gaiters, a bush hat, a neck-tie, a light nylon tracksuit for nights or extra daytime warmth.

Specialist clothing for mountain walking, such as thermal vests, windproof trousers, jackets and cagoules are available from outdoor equipment stores or mail order companies.

For further travels around Kenya, mountain gear is not so useful and other clothes may be more appropriate. When game-viewing, or on bird-watching safaris, shirts, trousers and jackets of light durable cotton or synthetic material, in buff or green shades, are recommended. For walks in open lowland areas shorts are fine, although long trousers are better for thick grass or undergrowth, and are essential in the evening if mosquitos are in the air. Long-sleeved shirts provide extra protection, and sleeves can be rolled up during the day. For car journeys long trousers or a divided skirt tend to be more comfortable. If you really want to look the part, a sleeveless safari vest with plenty of pockets is comfortable and saves carrying a bag for money, sunglasses and film. If your mountain boots are too heavy for general use, a light pair of suede desert boots are cool and comfortable. Safari clothing and desert boots are available in Nairobi but are often locally made and of inferior quality. The Rohan range of clothes are ideal for general travelling, available direct (30 Maryland Rd, Tongwell, Milton Keynes, MK15 8HN, UK, Tel 0908 216655), from any of their chain of retail shops, or from other outdoor equipment stores and mail order suppliers. High quality safari clothing is available from Travelling Light (Morland House, Morland, Cumbria, CA10 3AZ, UK, Tel 09314 488). Their mail order catalogue contains a wide selection of safari clothes, bags and accessories. Travelling Light also has retail shops in Malmesbury, Wiltshire (Tel 0666 825550) and Bletchingley, Surrey (Tel 0883 743456).

It is important to wear suitable clothes for your time in Nairobi and other towns, as well as when on safari or in the mountains. A skirt or long trousers are generally worn, particularly in Muslim areas. Nothing looks more incongruous, and is so offensive to local sensibilities, than men and women wandering around the streets dressed in nothing more than running shorts, singlets and sandals. These types of clothes should be saved for the coast.

Rucksacks

A rucksack (also called a backpack, and often shortened to 'sack' or 'pack') is essential for carrying all your supplies and equipment. A poor quality or unsuitable rucksack will be an unnecessary burden and make your walking less pleasant.

All but the smallest rucksacks ('day-packs') should have a frame to support the main body of the rucksack to prevent sagging. If the main weight of the sack is kept high and forward it will be more stable and easier to carry. Rucksacks with internal frames have a number of advantages: with a large padded back to spread the load they tend to be more comfortable; they are also flexible, but at the same time stable, which makes them more suitable for walking up and down steep gradients. In warm conditions the body-hugging nature of this design can cause your back to sweat. Recent models are built using mesh and special foam, or have pads attached, allowing more air to flow between your back and the frame.

Rucksacks are generally made from texturised nylon in various weights which makes the sack stronger, although it also increases its overall weight. Remember that the rucksack is likely to suffer more during its journeys to and from the mountains, on bus roof-racks or in the backs of cars, than it will during the actual walking.

Most rucksacks are built with lumbar pads which protect the base of the spine. A firm-fitting, padded, waist strap will transfer more than half the weight from your shoulders to your hips. Specialist alpine climbing sacks are not usually fitted with pockets, but for walking on the mountains pockets are very useful for carrying items such as a water bottle, camera, hat and sun-cream. For general travelling, however, pockets make a sack bulkier which can cause problems on public transport and also be a temptation for pick-pockets. If using public transport, when travelling to and from the mountains, leave your pockets empty. A rucksack with removable pockets is most useful for the combination of travelling and walking in Africa.

When buying a new rucksack, check all the smaller features for strength and reliability as well as the material and overall design. Look at the seams, straps, buckles and zips. If you already have a rucksack, make sure everything is in good condition before you leave. A broken rucksack will be very hard to replace in Nairobi.

Another aspect to check when buying a rucksack is that it fits you correctly; a poor fitting sack (especially if it is too big) will be very uncomfortable. Some rucksacks are available with adjustable harness or waist belt systems while others are fixed. In either case, the waist strap should sit comfortably above your hips while the straps are on your shoulders. If the waist strap and lumbar pad come down onto your buttocks, or the harness straps do not sit comfortably on your shoulders, the rucksack is too big. Most manufacturers produce a range of rucksacks designed for men and women of different heights and builds.

When packing your rucksack keep the weight high and even. Light items such as your sleeping bag and clothes should go at the bottom of the sack while heavier items, such as your tent and stove, should go towards the top. Items that you will need during the day can be spread between the top and side pockets. Your sleeping mat can be attached to the outside of the sack or rolled round the inside to form an extra layer of protection. No rucksack is completely waterproof so pack all the important items in plastic bags to keep them dry and free from dust.

Tents

In most of the areas described in this book, with the exception of Mount Kenya and lodges or campsites near some of the other routes, accommodation facilities in the mountains are limited. A tent is therefore essential to provide privacy and comfort, a vital shelter from the elements and, in certain cases, a sufficient barrier between you and inquisitive wildlife.

Even on popular routes where accommodation is provided, a tent allows more freedom and flexibility. Some of the privately owned permanent camps must be booked in advance, while some of the public huts are crowded in the high season or in a bad state of repair. With a tent you can avoid these places and find your own secluded camping spot. A tent also means that you are not forced to stick to any rigid itinerary and can alter your programme if required. (Maybe the altitude has slowed you down, or maybe you want to spend more time just admiring the views...)

The size of the tent you use depends on the number of people planning to sleep in it and the level of comfort (as opposed to protection) required. A wide range of backpacking tents designed for a single camper, or for any number up to six or seven, is available. Whatever the size, a tent should be light, but remember that the lightest tents tend to be the smallest and in very small tents the simplest activities, like eating a meal,

A good selection of Maps and Guides for Kenya is available from:

**The Map and Guide Shop
122 Kings Cross Road
London WC1X 9DS
Tel: 071- 278 8276**

A good general map is *Nelles Kenya* (£5.95) and an excellent practical guide is *The Camping Guide to Kenya* (£8.95). Prices include p+p

Discover a Continent

Africa

EXPEDITIONS & ADVENTURE SAFARIS

In Tanzania, Kenya and throughout Africa to suit all tastes and budgets. From one week to twenty weeks, including Camping Safaris and Lodge Safaris, Gorilla and Chimpanzee Searches and much more. For brochure contact:

TRACKS

12 Abingdon Road, London W8 6AF
Tel: 071 937 3028

reading the map, or even getting into your sleeping bag, require skilful and delicate manoeuvres. This is acceptable for a few nights but if you plan to carry your tent on some of the longer routes, or intend using it for accommodation throughout your stay in Kenya, then the lack of space may become tiresome and impractical. So, when buying a tent, choose the smallest and lightest you can afford but make sure you (and your companion/s) are going to be comfortable inside it.

Lightweight backpacking tents are available in various designs with a very wide range of materials and additional features to choose from. Poles are either rigid (used for traditional style ridge tents) or flexible (for more modern tunnel or dome tents). Tunnel tents use flexible poles but still require pegs and guy ropes to be erected (e.g. Vango's Hurricane range). Dome tents use more poles and the geodesic principle to be 'free-standing', which makes them particularly useful on rocky or sandy ground (e.g. Wild Country's Quasar or Trisar). Pegs and guys are only required in extreme conditions or to arrange features which are not part of the main structure such as the entrance cover (or 'porch'). Generally, tunnel or dome tents are roomier than a ridge tent of the same weight. In windy conditions, a ridge tent can present a flat surface to the wind which can put great stress on the fabric and guys. Tunnel and dome tents generally have rounded surfaces and are designed to flex in the wind. On a tunnel tent, using parallel hoops, it is harder to keep the fabric taut in windy conditions than on a geodesic dome tent.

VANGO **FORCE TEN HURRICANE**

Adventure proven tents.
RIGHT IN THERE... OUT THERE.

FORCE TEN

HURRICANE

For details of the complete range of outdoor equipment contact
VANGO (SCOTLAND) LTD, 70 East Hamilton St. Ladyburn, Greenock, Scotland PA15 2UB. Tel: (0475) 44122.

Tents are generally constructed using two layers of fabric, the inner and the flysheet, to provide a good level of insulation and protection. The most commonly used fabric is a tear-resistant nylon (e.g. Ripstop), although some tents have cotton inners. Cotton allows more ventilation, so cuts down on condensation, but is heavier than nylon especially when wet. Modern tents of all designs have an integral sewn-in groundsheet which keeps out ground-water and insects. Ventilation is important in warm conditions to reduce condensation, but it is essential that all vents and openings are covered with mosquito netting. If your tent is not supplied with netting fit some yourself before you leave. Single layer tents made of breathable fabrics (e.g. Wild Country's Gemini range) are very light but require a temperature differential to force water moisture through the tent fabric. This is no problem in high, cold mountain areas, but if you are also visiting lower, more humid areas of Kenya, condensation may build up on the inside of the tent.

Make sure your tent can be assembled and put up quickly and easily. If the sun is dropping and it is beginning to turn cold on the High Cherangani, or if the afternoon rain is about to fall on Mount Kenya, you need to get your tent up as quickly as possible. If the flysheet can be erected first this prevents the inner becoming too wet. Some makes of tent have the inner attached to the fly by zips so that both layers can be erected at the same time.

Conditions on the mountains of Africa can put just as much stress and strain on your tent as in any other part of the world, so when buying a tent it is important to check that all the features are well made. If you are using your existing tent check that everything is in good condition before you leave. The seams should be overlapped and sealed. Stitching should be tight and neat especially in areas where the stress will be highest such as on zips, peg loops and pole sleeves. Rigid poles should not bend and flexible poles should be well sprung to keep the tent fabric at the correct tension.

Before buying a tent try to talk to other backpackers and get some first-hand comments about the advantages and disadvantages of the various designs and features.

Sleeping equipment

Sleeping bags are made from various fabrics, but the main distinction is between bags filled with feathers or down (fine feathers) and those with a synthetic filling. Down sleeping bags compress easily, making them less bulky to carry, and also 'loft' (fill out) well to provide a good layer of insulation. Various types of down, or mixtures of feather and down, are used with different degrees of compression and loft. Down bags lose much of their effectiveness when wet or damp.

Synthetic bags are slightly bulkier and heavier than down bags of the same insulation value, but retain most of their effectiveness when wet or damp. Different types of synthetic filling are available of varying weights and loft levels (e.g. Holofil, Qualofil). Fabrics used for the outside of sleeping bags tend to be made from light tear-resistant nylon (e.g. Ripstop). Inner linings are made from cotton (which is comfortable but heavy), nylon (which is light but uncomfortable next to the skin), or a synthetic material combining the best features of cotton and nylon (e.g. Pertex).

When buying a sleeping bag the most important feature to consider is the 'season rating' which indicates the warmth of the bag. A 1-season bag is designed for warm nights, while a 5-season bag is for mid-winter or extreme high-level camping. For mountain walking in Kenya a 3- to 4-season bag is generally suitable, although this may be too warm if you plan to travel beyond the mountains (e.g. to the coast) during your time in Kenya. The layer system described in the Clothing section on p42 works equally well for sleeping bags and can be very effective when walking and travelling in a country like Kenya which has wide regional temperature variations.

I have found that two 2-season bags, or a 3-season and a 1-season bag, used together is more flexible than a single bag. In cold conditions two bags provide more insulation than one bag of the same weight, and in warmer conditions you can just use one bag. For mountain walking in Kenya I used a Vango Quattro 3-season bag with a 1-season 'moonbag' and found this ideal. (Moonbags are light, compact and very reasonably priced. The inside of the outer layer of a moonbag is coated with a heat-reflective film which increases the bag's insulation capability.) This system concept is not new; some manufacturers produce sets of sleeping bags designed to be used in this way.

Your sleeping bag system can be made even more versatile by proper use of features such as hoods and zips. A bag with a hood that covers most of your head will retain significantly more body heat in cold conditions. (It is important, however, not to cover your face completely; leave a small breathing hole to allow moisture to escape and prevent condensation forming inside the bag.) Conversely, in warm conditions, a zip can be used as a vent (particularly if it opens from either end) to allow cool air to circulate. If your bag does have a zip, however, ensure that it has a good baffle to prevent warm air being conducted away from your body by the metal or plastic of the zip.

A sheet inner sleeping bag provides another useful layer of insulation or can be used alone on very warm nights. A sheet inner also saves the inside of your sleeping bag from becoming too dirty and, because it can be washed and dried more easily than the whole bag, is more hygienic.

In any sleeping bag the filling becomes compressed under your body during the night, so an extra layer of insulation is vital. Most walkers use a closed cell foam pad (e.g. Karrimat) to provide this vital layer of insulation and an extra degree of comfort. Pressure-blown foam is stronger and harder to compress than chemically-blown foam. Some very poor mats are available, cheap copies of the more established makes, so if buying a mat check that it will not compress or tear too easily. Other sleeping mat designs are available, including self-inflating models, or combinations of closed cell and inflatable pad. For most of the routes decribed in this book the weather conditions are unlikely to be extreme but, for the occasional unexpectedly cold nights, it is worth carrying an emergency 'space blanket', a sheet of silver material which reflects body heat. Various types are available: very small and light models, folding to a size no bigger than a bar of soap, are fragile and have a limited life; tougher versions, for repeated use, are slightly heavier and bulkier. Note that space blankets do not breathe and trapped body moisture can freeze in very cold conditions.

Cooking equipment

For walkers in Africa, a stove is a vital piece of equipment. You are advised not to rely on open fires as many routes cross areas where wood is not available, and rain makes wood difficult to ignite. Of more significance, it is important to remember that all over Africa trees are being destroyed faster than they can be replaced and whole regions are now devoid of trees, leading to problems such as erosion and desertification. Various schemes have been introduced to educate people about conserving wood and, while a few branches for a walker's fire will not turn Africa into a desert, it makes the aid workers' job more difficult if double standards are seen to exist.

Stoves use a variety of fuels, including petrol (gasoline), paraffin (kerosene), methylated spirits (meths), and liquid gas (butane or a butane/propane mix). They all have their own advantages and disadvantages.

Pressurized petrol stoves are easy to light and provide a good heat. Self-pressurized stoves need priming with petrol, meths or priming paste. The stoves usually run on low-grade petrol which is cheap and easy to buy. Lead-free petrol (or white gas) is not available in Kenya. Stoves designed for lead-free fuel can use leaded petrol but need frequent maintenance to prevent clogging. After priming, the stove's own heat keeps the petrol pressure at the correct level, so the heating process is more efficient if the stove is insulated from cold ground. A piece of old Karrimat is ideal.

Paraffin stoves also need priming, but meths or paste is essential. This fuel is called kerosene in Kenya and is cheap and readily available as local people use it for their own stoves. Kerosene is less volatile than petrol but is oily and burns with a dirty flame.

Stoves using methylated spirits require no priming and burn with a safe and steady flame (e.g. Karrimor's Trangia stove). Meths is available in chemists or hardware stores (30/- per litre, 1990).

Certain types of stove are available which are designed to run on petrol or paraffin (e.g. the Coleman Peak One, or MSR Whisperlight) or on petrol (leaded or unleaded), paraffin and even diesel (the MSR X-GK).

Liquid gas stoves designed for backpacking use small disposable cartridges of butane or propane/butane mix (e.g. Gaz). The most popular size of butane cartridge (size C206) is available in Nairobi for around 50/- (1990), but the very small Globetrotter cartridge (size GT106) and the Super C206 (which both use propane/butane mix) are not available in Kenya.

(Remember that it is not permitted to carry any fuel for any stove on aeroplanes.)

When choosing a stove to use while mountain walking in Kenya, bear in mind that a stove of simple construction is less likely to go wrong. Learn how to maintain your stove and carry any necessary spares.

A useful addition to carry with your stove is a windshield made from thin and pliable aluminium sheeting. This makes lighting your stove easier and saves fuel. A carefully positioned rucksack will do the job in an emergency but a proper windshield is more effective.

Add to your stove a fuel bottle, a lightweight set of cooking pots, a pan-grip, plates and cutlery, and you will be completely self-contained in the wilds. Cheap aluminium pots and various wooden cooking implements can be bought in markets and *dukas* (local shops) all over Kenya.

Water bottles and carriers

During the day it is important to keep drinking plenty of liquids to avoid dehydration. (For more details see the Keeping healthy section on p61.) A wide range of bottles made from heavy duty plastic or aluminium (e.g. Sigg) are available. Bottles are also available in Nairobi but may be of poorer quality.

For the mornings and evenings, when established at your camping place, a large collapsible water bag is very useful. These bags can hold enough water for your cooking and drinking needs and can be folded away during the day's walking. In dry periods, or for sections on the route with long gaps between water sources, they can be filled at the campsite to provide additional water during the walk. These bags are usually fitted with a carrying handle and a tap, and are available in various sizes made from polythene or heavy duty PVC.

A range of collapsible water bottles and bags coated in synthetic fabric are available made by Liquipak. These bags have straps or buckles attached so that they can be carried as a belt or small rucksack as well as inside a larger pack.

Water purification

Contaminated water can contain organisms which cause stomach upsets and diarrhoea, or more serious diseases such as dysentery, cholera, giardia, bilharzia and hepatitis A. In Nairobi and other large towns water is generally treated, although even here the chlorine supply is not always reliable, but in rural and mountain areas a clean supply can never be guaranteed. Even in the remotest areas the water supply may have been contaminated by humans or animals.

While only a small number of visitors suffer from serious disease, even a mild illness could ruin your walking holiday so it is very important to ensure that your water supplies are clean and reliable. Water can be boiled vigorously to make it safe, but at high altitudes water boils at a lower temperature which may not destroy all the organisms. This process is also very time consuming and wastes a lot of fuel.

To clear water of larger particles and organisms various types of portable filter are available. These range from simple filter bags, which cost about £7 in the UK, to efficient miniature pumps, (e.g. Katadyn Pocket Filter) which costs over £150.

For smaller organisms a purification agent, in the form of tablets or solution, can be used. Silver-based agents (e.g. Micropur) leave no taste but may not be totally effective against all protozoa, including giardia. Chlorine-based agents (e.g. Puritabs) are more effective but give the water an unpleasant taste. Iodine-based agents (e.g. Potable Aqua) are more effective against protozoa and do not leave an unpleasant taste but should not be used for prolonged periods.

A fairly recent innovation of interest to walkers is the Travel Well, a highly effective portable treatment device that leaves no residual chemicals in the water and eliminates all significant parasitic, bacterial and viral contaminations including E. coli (which causes diarrhoea), cholera and salmonella bacteria, polio viruses and the parasitic cysts which cause giardia. A lighter version of the Travel Well, called the PWP, is more suitable for walkers as it fits directly onto a water bottle. The Travel Well is available from SafariQuip (address below), British Airways Travel Clinics and large branches of Boots the Chemist. The Travel Well and the PWP are also available direct from the manufacturer; Pre Mac Ltd, 103 Goods Sation Road, Tunbridge Wells, Kent TN1 2DP, UK.

Note that none of the water treatment agents or devices mentioned here are available in Kenya.

Suppliers and checklists

Most of the lightweight camping and backpacking equipment mentioned in this chapter is available from outdoor equipment shops or mail order companies. For a good selection of specialist equipment SafariQuip (13A Waterloo Park, Upper Brook Street, Stockport, SK1 3BP, UK, Tel 061 429 8700) produce a comprehensive mail order catalogue suitable for independent walkers and travellers, and another for full-scale expeditions. Travel accessories specially selected as suitable for visitors to Kenya are also featured in the catalogue available from Travelling Light (Morland House, Morland, Penrith, Cumbria, CA10 3AZ, UK, Tel 09314 488).

The following list of all the items of equipment mentioned in this section, plus some other items required or highly recommended, will help you prepare for your mountain walking in Kenya.

Rucksack
Tent, poles/hoops, pegs
Sleeping bag(s), sheet inner, mat, emergency blanket
Stove, fuel bottle, windshield
Cooking pots, pan-grip
Plates, mug, sharp knife, fork, spoon
Water bottle/carrier
Water filter or purification tablets
Multi-blade penknife (e.g. Swiss Army knife)
Wash-kit and towel
Tent and clothes repair kit
Torch, batteries, candle, matches, lighter
Sunglasses, compass, maps, clear plastic mapcase.

Although mosquitos are not usually a problem at high altitudes, a mosquito net is very useful for when you are in lower regions and not using your tent. (For more information see the Malaria section on p66.)

First aid kit
For full details about keeping healthy when travelling, and professional advice about items for a first aid kit, visitors to Kenya should consult their doctor and read a good manual. *Travellers' Health* or *The Tropical Traveller* are recommended. (Full details in the Books section on p57.)

Readers may find the following list of items useful for walking or travelling in Africa:

aspirin/paracetamol
oil of cloves (for toothache)
lip salve, UV barrier cream
intensive care cream (for dry or cracked skin)
antihistamine cream (to soothe stings and bites)
mosquito repellent
anti-malaria pills
antiseptic powder and cream
sticking plasters
tubigrip bandages (easier to use and keep clean than conventional bandages)
anti-diarrhoea pills
antibiotics/antibacterials (see note below)
a pack of disposable syringes and clean hypodermic and stitching needles

It is not necessary to carry large amounts of medicines or lotions. Most of these items can be bought in Nairobi, although some are expensive.

Antibiotics and antibacterials can be used for treating a wide range of external and internal infections, but note that incorrect use of these drugs can reduce effectiveness or even be dangerous. Get advice from your doctor or health centre.

In the case of an accident you may need stitches or an injection. In remote areas syringes and needles can be scarce and may have been used more than once. This leads to contamination and various diseases can be transmitted. Having your own needles and syringes can reduce the chance of contracting a disease in this manner. Some transmission prevention packs are available which also contain a drip or transfusion needle and various dressings. Suppliers include British Airways Travel Clinics and SafariQuip and Survival Aids.

Wearers of spectacles or contact lenses should carry spares and cleaning materials.

Photography

The mountains of Kenya provide excellent conditions for photography. During the middle of the day, the harsh light of the sun tends to neutralize some colours or lessen the contrast, especially at high altitude. Morning and evening are the best times. As well as dramatic peaks, picturesque scenery, interesting people or buildings and (if you are quick or patient) colourful birds and fascinating wildlife, the air is usually clear and colours are heightened, which helps to produce exceptionally sharp and well defined pictures.

When taking pictures of people be very discreet or ask permission first. Some people will expect payment. If you think this is demeaning do not take the photo. Do not take pictures of soldiers, government buildings, police posts, or anything else that might be considered sensitive or strategic. You may be accused of spying and your camera and film will be confiscated.

Film is widely available in Nairobi camera shops at prices comparable to, or only slightly more than, those paid in Europe or America. Camera equipment, however, is more expensive and visitors should bring all they need. Make sure your camera is in good condition especially if it is a sensitive SLR rather than a robust instamatic. Because of the heat and humidity of Kenya's climate, camera batteries discharge rapidly and the contact points should be cleaned regularly. Direct hot sunlight can damage film and the camera itself and dust is another enemy; keep your camera in a strong dustproof bag when not in use and use a daylight filter to protect the lens.

Some shops keep film on the shelf for a long time, which may affect its quality. Buy from a shop with a good turnover. The following camera shop in Nairobi can be recommended for supply, developing and printing of colour, black and white and slide films, camera batteries, spares and repairs: Expo Camera Centre, near the 20th Century cinema, Mama Ngina Street, Tel 21797, 336121.

Maps

The Survey of Kenya (SK) is a government department responsible for publishing official maps. These are produced in a range of scales but of most interest to walkers is the Y731 series, at 1:50,000 (50M), and the Y633 series, at 1:100,000 (100M). Generally the 50M maps cover the southern, western and central areas, while the 100M maps cover the less densely populated northern and eastern areas. Also available is the Y503 series, at 1:250,000 (250M).

Although useful for topographical detail, many of these maps have not been resurveyed or updated since the 1960s and are very out of date. For example, town names have changed, forest has been cut down or planted, and new roads have been built while old ones are now disused. However, these maps are not essential as the maps in this book provide sufficient information.

In Nairobi, Survey of Kenya 'Tourist Maps' of the whole country and maps of several national parks are available in bookshops or from the Public Map Office on Harambee Avenue, near the Kenyatta International Conference Centre. For security reasons, the 50M and 100M scale maps are very difficult to obtain but, if the correct procedures are followed (and you have enough time to spare), it is possible for tourists to obtain the copies. The procedure is as follows:

1. Go to the Survey of Kenya offices which are in the area of Nairobi called Ruaraka, on the left side of the Thika Road as you leave Nairobi, near the drive-in cinema.

2. Report to reception and explain that you are a tourist wanting to buy a map. You will then be shown the appropriate office.

3. In the office you will be asked to write a letter, saying exactly which map(s) you require (area, series number and sheet number) and explaining why you want to buy the map. The reason 'I am a tourist, intending to walk/camp/visit this area' should be sufficient (applications can also be made by post to Survey of Kenya, PO Box 30046, Nairobi, but this method is less reliable than a personal visit). Leave an address where you can be contacted.

4. Your letter will be sent to the Department of Defence (DOD) for security clearance. This can take up to three weeks. The DOD then inform the SK if clearance has been allowed. The SK inform you by post that the map is ready for collection and send you a form granting 'authority to procure topographical maps'. This may take another two or three weeks.

5. You go back to the Ruaraka office, or to the Public Map Office, with your authorization, and buy your map/s (25/- each, 1990).

Note that some maps are out of stock, but it is very difficult to find out which maps are available until you have your authorization form.

The SK 50M and 100M maps are also available from the Ordnance Survey (OS) in Britain. This is a far simpler method of obtaining maps but, once again, not all the maps are in stock. For further details contact the Overseas Surveys Directorate, Ordnance Survey, Maybush, Southampton SO9 4DH, Tel 0703 792236. Orders can also be made through an official OS agent.

For areas covered in this book, information about specific map titles and numbers are included in the individual route descriptions.

Other maps of particular use for walking include:
Mount Kenya, Tourist Map and Guide, Scale 1:125,000, Worldmaps Series, Sheet No 2, (Ordnance Survey, UK);
Mount Kenya, Map and Guide, Scale 1:50,000, drawn and published by Andrew Wielochowski and Mark Savage, (West Col, UK), also available in Nairobi;
Mount Elgon, Map and Guide, Scale 1:50,000, drawn and published by Andrew Wielochowski, (West Col, UK), also available in Nairobi.

For general travel around Kenya, to and from the mountains, the following maps are generally available and recommended:
Kenya, Scale 1:1,100,000, Nelles Maps (Nelles Verlag, Germany);
Kenya Tourist Map, Scale 1:1,750,000 (Macmillan, Kenya);
Kenya and Northern Tanzania, Scale 1:1,000,000 Sheet No. SK 81 (Survey of Kenya), only available in Kenya.
I have found that no one map is completely accurate or reliable; for travelling around Kenya visitors are recommended to use two or three maps together. Note that railway stations marked on the map may be some distance away from the town or centre with the same name.

For visits to national parks and reserves, Survey of Kenya publish maps to the following: Amboseli, Marsabit, Meru, Samburu and Buffalo Springs, Shimba Hills,Tsavo East, Tsavo West.
Also available:
Masaai Mara National Reserve Map, (Macmillan, Kenya),
Amboseli National Park Map, (Macmillan, Kenya).

For wider travel around Africa:
Michelin Map of Africa, Central and South. Sheet No.955, Scale 1:4,000,000.

Books

As this book covers the specifics of mountain walking, readers are advised to use a more general guidebook which can provide a general impression of the country and all the necessary information about accommodation, travel, places to visit and things to do in areas outside the mountains. For wider travels, specialist interests and background reading a very wide choice of books is available. Listed here is a small selection of recommended titles.

General guidebooks
Kenya Insight Guide, Mohamed Amin (ed.), (Apa Publications, Singapore)
The Spectrum Guide to Kenya, Camerapix, (Moorland, UK)
Kenya, a visitors guide, Arnold Curtis, (Evans, UK and Kenya)
The Insider's Guide to Kenya, M and P Bond, (Moorland, UK)
Mombasa and the Kenya Coast, J Jewell, (Evans, UK and Kenya)

For budget and independent travel
The Rough Guide to Kenya, Richard Trillo, (Rough Guides, UK)
The Real Guide to Kenya, Richard Trillo, (Prentice Hall, USA)
Kenya, Geoff Crowther, (Lonely Planet, Australia)

For wider travels, to and from Kenya
Sahara Handbook, Simon and Jan Glenn, (Lascelles, UK)
Spectrum Guide to African Wildlife Safaris, (Moorland, UK)
Africa on a Shoestring, Geoff Crowther, (Lonely Planet, Australia)
Mountain Walking in Africa 2: Tanzania, Zimbabwe and Malawi, David Else
(Robertson McCarta, UK)
Backpacker's Africa, East and Southern, Hilary Bradt, (Bradt, UK)
East Africa Travel Survival Kit, Geoff Crowther, (Lonely Planet, Australia)
Backpacker's Africa, West and Central, David Else, (Bradt, UK)
West Africa Travel Survival Kit, Alex Newton, (Lonely Planet, Australia)

Specialist guidebooks
The Mountains of Kenya, Paul Clark, (Mountain Club of Kenya, Kenya)
    A guide to almost 100 mountain peaks in Kenya for peak-baggers and
intrepid walkers. The section on Mount Kenya is very brief.
Backpacker's Africa, East and Southern, Hilary Bradt, (Bradt, UK)
    A guide for budget travellers venturing off the beaten track with an
emphasis on hiking and natural history.
The Camping Guide to Kenya, David Else, (Bradt Publications, UK)
    Describes every campsite in Kenya; in towns, national parks, mountain
areas and on the coast, plus areas suitable for hiking and 'wild' camping.
Guide to Mount Kenya and Kilimanjaro, Iain Allen, (MCK, Kenya)
    Guide for mountaineers and technical climbers to Africa's two highest
mountains.
East Africa International Mountain Guide, A. Wielochowski, (West Col, UK)
    A selection of technical climbing and mountaineering routes on the
crags and big walls of East Africa. Includes a brief section on caving.

Travel and walking manuals
The A to Z Guide for Lightweight Travellers, Clive Tully, (Writer's Block, UK)
    Concise reference book with detailed advice on everything from air-
beds to zoom lenses, via clothes, hitch-hiking, snake bites, tickets...
The Traveller's Handbook, Melissa Shales (ed.), (Wexas/Trade and Travel
    Publications, UK)
    Encyclopaedic guide to every conceivable aspect of world travel for
tourists and adventurers. Regularly updated.
The Independent Guide to Real Holidays Abroad, Frank Barret, (Newspaper
    Publishing, UK)
    For enterprising and imaginative tourists, with a section on UK tour
operators with programmes in Kenya. (Order direct from publisher.)
Backpacking and Camping in the Developing World, (Wilderness Press, USA)
    The title is self-explanatory. The book is full of valuable advice and

sound practical information for mountain walkers and travellers.

The Backpacker's Manual, Cameron McNeish, (Oxford Illustrated Press, UK)
   A complete guide to walking and camping. Although not about African mountains, most of the practical information still applies.

Desert Hiking, Dave Ganci, (Wilderness Press, USA)
   A specific guide to walking in hot climates, mainly in American deserts but much of the advice is relevant for Africa too.

Sources of Information for Independent and Overland Travellers, a regularly updated booklet, and a list of specialized technical guides and expedition manuals, is available from The Expedition Advisory Centre, The Royal Geographical Society, London, Tel 071 581 2057.

Health guides
Traveller's Health, Dr Richard Dawood, (Oxford University Press, UK)
The Tropical Traveller, John Hatt, (Pan, UK)

Field guides
Field Guide to the Birds of East and Central Africa, John Williams, and *Field Guide to the Mammals of Africa*, Haltenorth and Diller, (Collins, UK)
   The classic guides. Widely acknowledged to be the most comprehensive and authoratitive of their kind.

Naivasha, Baringo and Bogoria, Jean Hartley (Evans, UK and Kenya)
   Concise and portable field guides to the flora and fauna in these three Rift Valley lakes.

Background reading
Many hundreds of books have been written about all aspects of life and travel in Kenya. Below is a very small selection of highly recommended and particularly relevant titles to provide background information or to get you in the mood before you leave:

Mount Kenya, John Reader, (Elm Tree Books, UK)
   A personalized account of the author's walk from the farmland and foothills, through the forest and moorland, to the peak area, and finally a climb to the summit of Nelion. A good selection of photos captures Mount Kenya in all its moods.

Snowcaps on the Equator, Clive Ward, Iain Allen, Gordon Boy, (Bodley Head, UK)
   Excellent photographs of Africa's dramatic and mysterious equatorial mountains, including Mount Kenya, Mount Elgon, the Aberdares and several of Kenya's northern peaks. Evocative background essays provide more than enough inspiration for walkers considering a trip to the mountains of East Africa.

Journey to the Jade Sea, John Hillerby, (Paladin/Collins, UK)
   A walk with camels through the deserts and mountains of northern Kenya.

No Picnic on Mount Kenya, Felice Benuzzi, (Kimber, UK)

Gripping and inspiring account of three Italian prisoners of war attempting to reach the summit of Mount Kenya.

Different Drums, Michael Wood, (Century Hutchinson, UK)

Reflections on a changing continent and its peoples by the founder of the African Flying Doctors, with striking photographs.

For more advice and information about maps, guides and travel books about Kenya contact a good bookshop such as McCarta (122 King's Cross Rd, London, Tel 071 278 8276), Stanfords (Long Acre, Covent Garden, London, Tel 071 836 1321), or The Travel Bookshop (Blenheim Crescent, London W11, Tel 071 229 5260). For a complete list of books, journals and papers written about all aspects of Kenya (mainly of academic interest but including general interest books and works of literature) readers should consult the Kenya volume of the World Bibliographical Series, published by Clio Press, Oxford, and available in large reference or university libraries. For a very wide selection of secondhand and out of print books about early exploration, history, landscape, wildlife, peoples, and all aspects of East and Central Africa, all available by mail order, contact Risborough Books (81 Manor Park Ave, Princes Risborough, Aylesbury, HP17 9AR, UK, Tel 08444 3165). For natural history titles, all available by mail order, contact the Natural History Book Service (2 Wills Rd, Totnes, Devon TQ9 9XN, UK, Tel 0803 865913). Trailfinders' Kensington High Street branch in London has an information centre and library for customers (Tel 071 938 3366).

Nairobi has several good bookshops stocking a wide selection of fiction, guides and 'coffee-table' books.

Britain's leading travel and expedition supplier

SAFARIQUIP

−Helpful
−Friendly
−Showroom
−Mail Order
−Free Catalogue
−Free Advice
Call us now!

For selected travel goods and expedition equipment

13A Waterloo Park, Upper Brook Street, Stockport SK1 3BP
Telephone 061−429 8700   Fax 061−429 8837

On The Mountains

Keeping healthy

Three main factors which can adversely affect the health of the mountain walker in Africa are the water supply, the temperature and the altitude. Lack of water can result in dehydration while the micro-organisms carried in unclean water can cause various diseases. Low temperatures can lead to chills or exposure, and walkers climbing mountains too quickly can suffer from altitude sickness. However, despite these potential dangers, problems can be reduced or completely avoided by taking certain precautions which are usually a combination of careful preparation before you leave home and sound common sense while you are on the mountain routes.

Comprehensive information on health and safety when mountain walking (or about general travelling through other regions) in Africa can be found in a number of specialized reference books (see Books section on p57), but the following sections provide some basic information.

Water and dehydration

On many of the mountains described in this book daytime conditions are very warm which means walkers will perspire considerably. If a breeze is blowing you may not even notice the sweat, as the moisture evaporates as soon as it reaches the surface, but it is most important to replace these lost fluids by drinking plenty of liquid. Even during cold or wet weather on the mountains you will still perspire more than usual.

If lost fluids are not replaced you could begin to suffer from dehydration. The first symptom of dehydration is, obviously, thirst. If your condition becomes worse you may stop sweating and your urine will turn dark orange. In extreme conditions your skin becomes puffy and you may find it difficult to swallow. Dehydration also affects your mental capacities, leading you to make irrational decisions.

These symptoms are easily avoided if your liquid intake is correct. This varies according to the altitude and your own level of exertion but, even on fairly gentle walks, you should drink two to three litres of liquid per day, or more in very warm conditions. If your urine turns dark, or if you are not urinating, this indicates that your intake level is too low.

Every member of a walking group should carry, at the very least, one litre each for the period between camps, or three times this amount if water is not guaranteed at the next night's camp. The following system is useful and convenient: a litre of liquid at breakfast (tea, fruit juice or water), another litre during the day's walking (usually water and increased if a spring or stream is passed), and another litre in the evening (tea or cocoa). The caffeine in tea and coffee encourages urination which reduces the amounts of fluid absorbed by your body. Herb teas or decaffeinated coffee avoid this but are not available in Kenya. Fruit drink crystals and tins of drinking chocolate, cocoa and Milo are easy to find and make ideal mountain drinks.

It is also important to ensure that the water you are drinking is clean and free from contamination. Even on the remotest mountain the water may contain some of the organisms which cause diarrhoea (which can lead to dehydration) or more serious diseases. While innoculations provide a certain level of protection they do not give you complete immunity. Walkers are advised to use a purification agent or filtering device (see the Equipment section p52).

Temperatures

Night falls quickly in Africa and on African mountains the temperature can also fall very fast. A drop in air temperature leads to a drop in your body temperature which, in turn, can lead to a serious chill. Therefore it is important to keep your body warm whenever the conditions start to get cold.

At the end of the day's walking, or even if you stop for a short rest during the day, put on at least one other layer of clothing. This is especially important if you have been sweating or if your back is wet after being in contact with your rucksack. Do not wait until you feel cold; do it as soon as you stop.

Serious problems resulting from chills are unlikely to affect walkers but, in emergencies or unexpected situations, continued exposure to cold temperatures can lead to hypothermia. Sufferers may be unable to move or completely lose consciousness. The most important thing to do is raise the body temperature. All wet and cold clothing should be removed and the sufferer placed inside a tent and as many sleeping bags as are available. If a tent cannot be pitched the wind should be kept off by using a space blanket, cagoules or the tent fabric. A second person can get into the sleeping bag to provide more warmth.

Extreme conditions can also lead to frostbite. This is more likely to affect climbers rather than walkers, but at high altitudes night

How to reach the three highest peaks in Africa

Mt Stanley
Mt Kenya
Kilimanjaro
081-577 7187

Discover the sights, sensations and experiences of Kenya, Tanzania and the Ruwenzori with

SHERPA
E X P E D I T I O N S
Mountain Walking Holidays Worldwide
131a Heston Rd, Hounslow, Middx.

Snow on Mt Kenya's peaks   *Giraffe near Mt Suswa*

temperatures can drop to below freezing point so walkers should be aware of potential dangers. In very cold conditions the body's extremeties (especially toes and, to a lesser extent, fingers) can literally freeze. This can be avoided by using appropriate footwear and gloves, and changing wet socks. Keep your boots and socks inside your tent at night to stop them freezing and keep them warm for the next day's walking.

If walking in wet and cold conditions a second pair of shoes, for using around the camp in the evenings, gives your feet a chance to dry out. This also helps to prevent blisters as wet and cold feet are more susceptible to chafing. Some walkers put their boots inside a canvas bag right inside their sleeping bag to keep them dry and warm. (A plastic bag prevents moisture from escaping.)

Altitude

For mountain walkers the most important factor to consider is the effect of altitude and this is frequently overlooked by visitors to Kenya. Even the altitude of Nairobi, at 1500m/5,000ft, is noticed by new arrivals who normally live in lower regions.

The effects of altitude become particularly noticeable, and potentially more serious, as you start walking at altitudes of more than 3000m/10,000ft above sea level. More important than the altitude itself, though, is the rate at which it is gained. If you are unacclimatized and gain height too quickly you are much more likely to suffer.

Do not rush your walking. Lower approach routes are often straightforward and it can be tempting to walk and gain height too rapidly. If you avoid the lower section of a route by driving you can help the acclimatization process by spending two nights at the roadhead, or at another point on the route, rather than heading directly for the high peaks. If you feel tired heed your body's warning and rest for a day. This may be difficult if you are with an organized group on a time-table, but it is especially easy for self-contained walkers who can pitch a tent almost anywhere.

Experienced mountain walkers all over the world keep to the following guidelines: above 3500m/11,500ft, height gain should average 500m/1,500ft per day, with a rest day every three days. Even if you ascend more than 500m during the day, try to descend to a point within the guidelines for your night's sleep.

The effects of altitude can take a number of forms, all loosely termed 'altitude sickness'. Every year on Mount Kenya, however, several people are affected, so walkers should be aware of the symptoms.

The first symptoms of altitude sickness are lethargy, headaches, vomiting, complete loss of appetite and extreme tiredness. Even at rest your pulse rate will be very fast and you may have difficulty sleeping. If these symptoms persist you should descend to a hut or suitable camping spot and rest there until your body has acclimatized and the symptoms have stopped.

If these early symptoms are ignored, and you continue to gain height, the condition is likely to get worse. You may suffer from pulmonary oedema, where excess fluid collects in the lungs. Symptoms include all the early symptoms outlined above plus breathlessness and a gurgling sound from the lungs. A sufferer may start to cough up foamy mucus. Cerebral oedema, which puts pressure on the brain, can be equally as serious; symptoms include severe headache, hallucinations and lack of coordination.

Don't let these descriptions put you off. If you adhere to the guidelines you are unlikely to suffer heavily from the effects of altitude.

Taking aspirin or paracetamol may help to reduce headaches caused by altitude, but if these headaches persist or get worse do not try to overcome them by taking more pills. A drug called Diamox is available which reduces some of the effects of altitude sickness, but if the early symptoms are disguised you may suffer more seriously higher up the mountain.

At high altitudes the atmosphere is thin and only filters a small amount of the sun's ultraviolet light. To protect against burning use a good UV barrier cream or sun blocker. Good quality sunglasses, that reduce UV and visible light, are also recommended.

General health and hygiene

Some water-borne diseases can also be transmitted through food or dishes that have been infected with contaminated water. When eating in hotels and restaurants, wherever possible make sure that the food is well cooked and avoid salads, raw seafood or fruit that has already been peeled. In the small snack bars serving local food you can often actually see the food being freshly cooked.

It is often easier for mountain walkers, camping in wilderness regions, to keep healthy than for tourists staying at hotels. You can ensure that your own food is well cooked and can check the purity of your water supply. It is important to eat properly when walking and travelling. Do not allow your menu to become repetitive or boring. When situations allow, be adventurous with local foods or spices. An interesting meal, with a number of courses or, at the very least, more than one type of food on the plate, is more psychologically appetizing.

It is worth noting that the most common problem for visitors to foreign countries is travellers' diarrhoea, which is often not a symptom of any disease, but rather a result of your body being submitted to unusual foods, temperatures or conditions. In most cases you become used to the changes and the trouble clears up after a few days. During a severe attack it may be difficult to eat solid food, but it is important to keep drinking fluids, especially in the mountains. Oral rehydration salts can be added.

Remember that your own personal hygiene is also very important. Wash your hands well before eating or preparing food. Keep cuts or grazes clean and covered to prevent infection. Medicated soap can further reduce the chance of infection and a small nail scrubbing brush is useful. Biodegradable soap and detergent avoids further polluting water sources. This can be bought from specialist outdoor suppliers, or any good shop selling environmentally sound items, but is not available in Kenya.

If porters are preparing your food try to encourage them to wash their hands too. Be gently persuasive and explain that their cleanliness is important for your health (as well as theirs) and for the success of the walking tour.

When you go to the toilet move well away from paths, campsites and water sources. Dig a hole with a stick and bury your excrement and toilet paper; covering it with a stone is not enough. Better still, take some matches with you and burn the paper immediately after use. Some campsites, particularly on Mount Kenya, have become horribly contaminated by thoughtless walkers. On the less well-known routes conditions are still acceptable and it is the prime responsibility of all walkers to do everything they can to maintain this.

Some campsites have also been spoilt by large amounts of rubbish, especially tins. Avoid carrying too many tins of food on your mountain walking trip. Fresh vegetables and dried foods in paper bags and packets are no heavier and more convenient. Paper and card can be burnt, but this should be done thoroughly and the ashes buried in a deep hole. Merely covering rubbish with loose earth is not enough. Do not bury tins, aluminium foil and plastic bags as these take many years to decompose, pollute the soil, and may be dug up by animals who could then injure or choke themselves. Despite evidence to suggest that numerous walkers and campers believe tins and foil to be combustible, these items will not burn, so do not try to destroy them on a fire. It is better to bring ALL your rubbish off the mountain. Tins can be flattened to reduce space. Take a strong plastic bag specially for collecting waste. Encourage porters not to dispose of waste thoughtlessly. On the last day of your walking, if you can bring down some of the rubbish left behind by less considerate visitors, then you will be doing a great favour for other walkers and for the mountains themselves.

Mountain walkers in Kenya are unlike many tourists, who come only to visit the coast or the national parks. The other tourists come merely to take what the country offers, and their presence can lead to the eventual destruction of much of Kenya's natural resources. However, mountain walkers, if they adopt the responsible attitudes previously referred to, can contribute positively to the protection of Kenya's natural resources by ensuring that their own presence has 'minimum impact' on the mountain environment. Readers interested in the importance and further implications of the concepts of minimum impact and responsible tourism should contact Tourism Concern, a UK-based organization whose aims include the promotion of greater understanding of the effects of tourism on host communities and environments (8 St Mary's Terrace, Ryton, NE40 3AL, Tel 091 413 5393).

The recently formed Mount Kenya Conservation Committe, an organization consisting of the National Park authorities, Naro Moru River Lodge, Mountain Rock (Bantu) Lodge and the National Outdoor Leadership School, have been encouraging and promoting cleanliness and conservation on the mountain's popular routes. Their work is very valuable and should be supported.

Malaria
The malaria parasite is carried by the female anopheles mosquito, but in regions above 2000m this species is unlikely to be found. However, a malaria prophylaxis is advisable, especially if you are visiting a lowland region where malaria is more of a risk, during your time in Kenya.

It is always better to avoid being bitten than rely on the prophylaxis for protection. During the evenings, when mosquitos are in the air, wear trousers and long-sleeved shirts to keep your legs and arms covered , and use a repellent cream or lotion. Some travellers have found that the traditional Eastern method of eating garlic to create a body odour which repulses mosquitos to be very effective. This is particularly useful in parts of East Africa, including Kenya, where the malaria parasite has developed a resistance to certain prophylactics. (Garlic is available in Kenya.)

When camping, your tent should be fitted with netting across the ventilation openings. Air can circulate without mosquitos and other insects entering. If you are sleeping out in the open, or in a hotel or B & L, a mosquito net that covers your sleeping bag or bed is very useful. (Mosquito nets treated with insecticide are also useful for keeping away very small insects such as sand-flies.) A number of portable lightweight nets are available from specialist outdoor equipment shops or mail order companies. A wide range of high quality mosquito nets is available from Swiss Net UK (Thornfield Industrial Estate, Nottingham, UK, Tel 0602 503403).

Safety and security

Accidents, emergencies, and mountain rescue

Apart from Mount Kenya, most of the mountain regions of Kenya are not developed for recreational walking and walkers on the peaks and highland areas are unlikely to meet other tourists. This remoteness also means that it is more difficult to get help in case of accident or emergency. It is highly recommended not to walk alone on the mountains of Kenya.

There is no public ambulance service in Kenya. Make sure your insurance covers you for emergency transport inside Kenya as well as for the flight home. If an urgent rescue is required, the Flying Doctor Service of East Africa can provide its members with emergency treatment and air transport. Annual membership is US$20 for adults. Temporary membership for tourists is US$10 for one month. For more information contact the Flying Doctors Society of Africa, Wilson Airport, PO Box 30125, Nairobi, Tel 501301, or contact their overseas representatives at PO Box 50756, Montecito CA 93150, USA, or the African Medical Research Foundation, Bristol, UK, Tel 0272 238424.

If a member of your walking party is injured and unable to move, divide the remainder of the group so that while help is being sought the injured person is not left alone. If only two people are in the group the person going for help should take very careful note of the injured person's position. A bright piece of clothing can be tied to a rock or tree to act as a landmark. In hot conditions ensure the injured person has sufficient liquids. In cold temperatures leave a sleeping bag, erect the tent or arrange some shelter. If sending a porter or local person to fetch help from a park ranger station, police station or other point with transport or radio contact, emphasize the urgency of the situation and, to avoid confusion, write all the details of the accident on paper for the messenger to deliver. A promise of reward for prompt action would be appropriate.

On Mount Kenya the park rangers will be able help move an injured person if necessary. Stretchers are stored at park gates and at the ranger station in the Teleki Valley. Rangers are not able to carry out technical rescues for mountaineers and rock climbers in difficulties, although they will alert and assist the Mountain Club of Kenya mountain rescue team which is based in Nairobi. In the other mountain national parks most gates and ranger stations have radios to summon help if required, and rangers will help where possible, although their facilities are likely to be limited. Any porters or rangers who do help in an emergency should be rewarded for their help.

Theft and robbery

Walkers in the mountains of Kenya are unlikely to experience any kind of security problems. Generally, the local people in remote mountainous regions will greet visitors with interest and friendliness, or possibly with indifference, but unpleasant or hostile behaviour is virtually unknown.

If you are walking in a populated mountain region it is advisable to ask permission before camping near villages or small *centres* (settlements). In rural centres walkers may be allowed to camp in the grounds of a police post, mission or school. You may be visited by inquisitive children who may be tempted to pilfer from your camp - keep small and attractive items out of reach. A smile and a few words of Swahili will go a long way in situations like this. (Avoid giving children money or sweets, if asked for, as this sets a bad precedent and walkers coming after you are likely to be pestered for more.)

In some places, even remote areas, it may not be advisable to leave a car unattended for long periods. Usually it is possible to leave a car at a farm, mission, shop, police post, or school. Permission should be sought and a small 'fee' is appropriate. Points where this is applicable are indicated in the relevant sections.

In Nairobi, and in other large towns where tourists are not an uncommon sight (e.g. Mombasa and Malindi) the problems of harrassment or robbery are more serious. Just as in any large city in the world certain parts of Nairobi should be avoided, especially at night. Keep away from dark back streets and parks. Robberies are not uncommon in Nairobi's Uhuru Park, where unsuspecting tourists taking an evening stroll are easily pounced upon.

Even some areas outside Nairobi cannot be regarded as totally safe. Robberies have occurred on the Ngong Hills and at Fourteen Falls and Ol Doinyo Sapuk near Thika, both popular weekend and evening picnic spots.

The only other security problem that might be encountered by walkers on the mountains is pilfering by porters. Almost without exception the porters hired officially through lodges, or those employed by companies organizing walking tours, are totally trustworthy and reliable, and very few incidents of theft have occurred. Occasionally, however, porters may sub-contract out their work to less reliable colleagues. To avoid unnecessary temptation it is always best to keep your valuables with you. It is a good idea to keep a small day-pack anyway to carry food, water and spare clothing.

Walkers exploring remote mountain regions have employed as porters local people for whom this work is an unexpected event, and are inclined to take too much advantage of their position. Large scale theft is never a problem but on some occasions small items such as food or medicine, or maybe a knife or water bottle, may go missing. No real malice is intended but walkers employing porters in this informal manner should guard against such situations. Stress from the start that your baggage is not to be tampered with and keep your valuable items in your day-pack.

Danger from animals
In the mountains of Kenya walkers are more likely to have potentially dangerous encounters with animals than with humans. Even so, wild animals of all kinds (including snakes) usually try to avoid contact with

humans and will often move away at the sound of your approach. If you do find yourself walking near a herd of buffalo or elephant all you are likely to see are piles of dung, rustling branches and (if you are lucky) a glimpse of a grey tail-end disappearing into the bush.

An animal that is suddenly confronted, and with no apparent means of escape, is likely to be aggressive so it is advisable not to walk too quietly through bush or forest country and give animals sufficient warning of your approach.

If you unexpectedly meet a large animal, such as a solitary elephant or lion, and it shows no sign of moving away, it is important to keep absolutely still and quiet. Do not run unless there is a tall, strong, easy-to-climb tree very close at hand. Back away slowly, making no movement or sound that could be misinterpreted as a threat. Buffalo are very unpredictable, especially old males who have been forced out of their herd. If a lone buffalo sees or smells you it is likely to charge. Experienced mountain and bush walkers say that in cases like this it is best not to run, but rather crawl (or 'run like a rat') around the stumps of trees and bushes making it harder for the buffalo to reach you with its horns.

Of course, it is far better to avoid a situation like this in the first place. In areas where encounters with wildlife are likely a local guide is particularly recommended. Local people are usually more attuned to conditions in the forest or bamboo and able to help you avoid any dangerous encounters. Areas where guides are recommended and where thay can be hired are described in more detail in the individual route descriptions. Never attempt to creep up on large, potentially dangerous, animals unless you are with an experienced guide or ranger.

Animals are most likely to be a problem at night when you are camping. Your campsite may be visited by scavengers of different types; rats, mice and hyraxes on the high ground, and monkeys or baboons in the forested regions. These animals may be attracted by the smell of fresh food, so it is important not to leave unfinished or unsealed food lying loose around the campsite. Everything should be well wrapped and kept inside the doorway or porch of your tent. Never keep freshly smelling food (e.g. an opened tin of corned beef) inside your tent.

You may hear gazelle, hyena or even buffalo wandering past your site in the night but your tent is unlikely to be touched or damaged.

In popular areas of Kenya (such as national parks) some animals, including baboons and hyenas, have become unafraid of humans and will enter campsites at night specifically to search for food. Baboons have been known to rip tents open to reach unwrapped or strong smelling food stored inside. In the mountain areas described in this book problems of this nature are not usually encountered.

Flora and fauna

For all visitors to Kenya the sheer variety of the flowers, trees, insects, birds and animals of Africa are a constant source of interest. It is a subject far too wide to describe fully in this book, and all visitors to Kenya are strongly advised to carry a good field guide covering the flora or fauna of particular interest to them. (See the Books section on p57 for more details.) The short sections below provide a brief introduction.

Vegetation
Walkers on the mountains of Kenya pass through various zones of vegetation, which form roughly concentric rings around the mountain, varying as height is gained and local weather conditions change.

The lower slopes of most mountains, above 1500m/5,000ft, have been cleared of natural vegetation and are farmed by the local people. You will probably see maize, bananas and other crops growing on *shambas* (smallholdings), or possibly tea and coffee on small plantations.

Beyond the farmland, usually at about 2000m/6,500ft, walkers reach the first zone of natural vegetation - the forest. Air rises and cools when it reaches the mountain region and the consequent condensation results in rainfall. Because this rainfall is localized, and not necessarily part of a larger climate pattern, this vegetation zone is termed high altitude rain forest. The main species found here are cedar, olive and podocarpus.

At around 2500m/8,200ft the forest gives way to bamboo. Huge bushes grow closely together to form a dense impenetratable barrier. Walkers usually follow clear paths which have been cut through the bamboo. Less well defined trails branching away from the main path have probably been created by large animals such as elephant or buffalo and should not be followed.

The bamboo thins out at about 3000m/10,000ft, and walkers will pass through heath and moorland scenery. At these heights walkers will see species of plant unique to the mountains of Africa; in the heathland are clumps of giant heather which are high enough to get lost in, while on the moorlands are unique Afro-alpine plants, specially adapted to survive in extremes of climate, like the tall feathery 'ostrich plume' lobelias and giant tree groundsels, which look like cabbages on poles. The dry leaves of old groundsels rattle and scrape in the wind making an eerie sound on a dark deserted mountainside.

At around 4000m/13,000ft the conditions are too dry and cold for most plants to grow, and the vegetation thins out completely leaving only mosses and lichens to cover the bare rocks.

Mammals
The various vegetation zones outlined above form a variety of habitats for an even wider variety of animals and birds.

Among the large species inhabiting the mountain forests are the giant forest hog, buffalo and elephant. Elephant populations have been severely reduced in recent years by poaching. Other mammals likely to be seen in the forest are waterbuck, baboon, bongo, duiker and monkey. Numerous species of monkey inhabit this zone but the most easily recognized is the colobus with its distinctive black and white shaggy appearance and barking call, heard particularly at dusk and dawn.

The buffalo and elephant often move up into the bamboo zone, or even on occasion to the moorland regions. In these zones you may also see bush pig, duiker, eland, bushbuck and gazelle, although often only a fleeting glimpse as the animal runs for cover. Lion and leopards also inhabit these zones but you will be very lucky (or unlucky!) to see more than a set of footprints. In the high alpine zones, on any rocky or grassy area and around the mountain huts, rock hyrax and grass rats are common.

Birds

On the mountains of Africa most birds are forest species although some are unique to the moorland areas. The main families are the bulbuls and warblers. Francolins, weaver birds, hornbills and turacos are often seen.

In the forest zones, one of the most commonly sighted birds is the bright green malachite sunbird. These birds feed on the nectar of flowers and assist in pollination by carrying the pollen from one flower to another. Also seen, especially on Mount Kenya, is the slender-billed chestnut-wing starling, a dark blue bird easily identified in flight by its long tail and bright wing patches.

The moorland provides a habitat for rats and mice and so attracts birds of prey including the red-tailed augur buzzard, the white-necked raven and Mackinder's eagle owl. Near the summits of even the highest mountains alpine swifts can usually be seen.

SPECIAL CAMPING SAFARIS LTD

ECONOMICAL LANDROVER AND TRUCK SAFARIS
Groups, Schools, Clubs, Families; Our 4 wheel drive vehicles are available to take you on the safari of your own design Ask for Mike or Marie-Louise.

* **Masai Mara—4 Days**
* **Amboseli & Tsavo—4 Days**

Our speciality / Oze specialiteit;
* *10 day expeditions to*
* **Turkana East**
* **Mt. Kenya, Samburu, Rift Valley & Mara**
* **Walking Safaris**
* **Horse Riding Safaris**
* **Tanzania—5 days**
* **Climbing Mt. Kenya—4 days**

Departures every Wednesday & Sunday.

FREE T-SHIRT WITH EVERY <u>DIRECT</u> BOOKING
Visit us at: Gilfillan House, (next to African Heritage), Kenyatta Avenue.
P.O. Box 51512 Nairobi, Kenya Telex: 25260 "CLOGGY KE"
Tel: 338325/20072 (office) 882541 (home).
Fax: 333448 ATTN: SPECIAL CAMPING SAFARIS

Part Two

ROUTE DESCRIPTIONS

Introduction

Route descriptions: Most route descriptions are described as for an ascent. Walkers going up and down the same route can usually retrace their steps to find their way back. For walkers traversing a mountain, coming up one route and going down another, route descriptions cannot simply be read in reverse. Landmarks, features, and even the routes themselves often appear very different and walking times will also differ. Thus, where necessary, routes are described in both directions.

Times and distances: Walking times, rather than distances, are given as part of each route description. These walking times are given in days for the route as a whole, or in hours between main points along the route. Strip diagrams show the time in hours and minutes between obvious features and landmarks. When planning your day's walking allow extra time for rests, lunch, photo stops, etc. On the lower approach routes, and on the sections open to vehicles, distances and driving times are also given.

All times given are average times. Fit and well-acclimatized walkers, familiar with the conditions on African mountains, will be able to cover the distances in a shorter time, while other walkers may take longer. Do not feel that you are 'falling behind schedule'. Allow for extra hours, or an extra day if necessary, and be sure that you are properly prepared; take adequate food and water, and enough supplies to ensure safe and enjoyable walking throughout the day.

Heights: In the route descriptions heights are given in metres and feet. For convenience heights are rounded to ten, except for summits and other important features.

Where the time in hours is given between main points along the route the gain in height (above 300m) is also indicated. This helps walkers to plan their ascents allowing sufficient time for acclimatization.

Terminology: Various terms are used in the route descriptions which may require further definition: a **track** is not surfaced or graded but is generally passable for vehicles; a **path** is generally clear to follow; a **trail** is indistinct, often created by animals and followed by walkers when convenient; a **way** is a general direction which must be followed when the path or trail is very indistinct or non-existent.

Techniques: Except on very popular routes (e.g. on Mount Kenya) even a 'clear path' will not be like the well-trodden and waymarked paths in European or North American areas geared for recreational walking. Walkers should not always expect to follow an obvious single path; some routes may involve following vague animal trails through thick bamboo, while others will require walkers to rely on their map, compass and sense of direction to get between one major feature and the next. When on out-and-back routes you should learn to remember landmarks; turn round and look back occasionally on your way out so that you will recognize these again more easily on the return. If it helps you remember, make a list as you go along.

Best times to visit: In each chapter the best seasons to visit the individual mountains have been described. The climate of Kenya, along with many other parts of the world, is becoming increasingly harder to predict, and walkers should be flexible and prepared for all conditions.

Porters and guides: Porters can help to lighten your load especially if you plan to spend several days in the mountains. This is particularly useful for walkers who may not be acclimatized. Guides are very useful in areas where routes may be unclear. Their local knowledge of route conditions, water points, and the chances of encountering wild animals is invaluable. Unless otherwise arranged, porters and guides will provide and carry their own food and water. Porters do not provide their own rucksacks and tents.

On Mount Kenya porters and guides, if required, can easily be arranged, usually through a hotel or lodge. In other, less frequented, areas porters and guides are not generally available. Full details are given in each chapter.

National parks: Mount Kenya, the Aberdare Range, Longonot, Hell's Gate and a section of Mount Elgon have been gazetted as national parks. Gates are usually positioned where approach routes cross the park boundary, which are manned by rangers and park officials, and all visitors must pay for the number of days they spend in the park. For non-citizens this is 200/- ppd (1990). Camping is included in this fee, but hut fees must be paid separately. (Full details in each chapter.) Vehicles must also be paid for. Porters and guides enter at the citizens rate. If you are hiring porters or guides check if their price includes park entrance fees.

The number of days you spend in the park are generally paid for in advance. Keep all your receipts and tickets especially if you plan to enter by one gate and exit by another. If you do decide to stay in the park for longer than originally intended extra days can be paid for when you leave.

Maps: The route maps have been specially drawn for this book, and only features of importance to walkers are included. Contour lines are at 200m intervals (650ft) except where essential topographical features need to be indicated. On area maps only the main approach routes described in the text and other important features are shown.

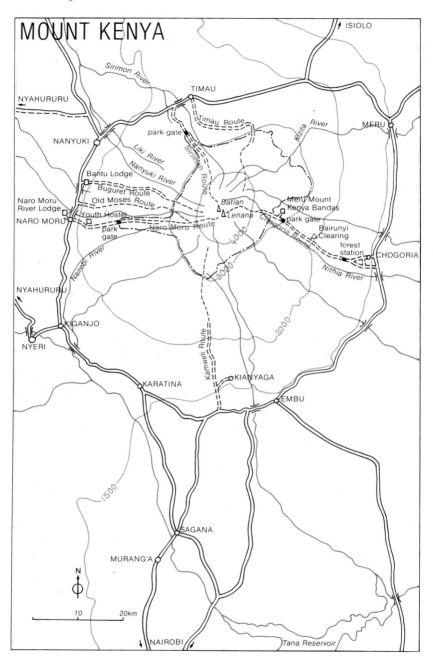

Mount Kenya

Mount Kenya is the highest mountain in Kenya and the second highest in Africa after Kilimanjaro. The main peaks stand at the high central point of a large, roughly circular, massif rising from around 2000m (7,000ft) to over 5100m (17,000ft) at the summits, and some 50km in diameter. The twin summits, Batian and Nelion, require technical climbing on rock or ice but Point Lenana, the third peak at 4985m, can be reached by walkers and is a popular goal for most visitors to the mountain.

Many walkers, unused to the conditions on high African mountains, feel they have 'failed' if they do not reach Point Lenana and forget that Mount Kenya also offers a wide variety of fascinating routes through high moor and heathland and around the valleys and ridges that radiate out from the main peaks.

This radial pattern of ridges and valleys is the result of glacial erosion. Mount Kenya was originally a volcano, and the peaks are the remains of the hard central plug, but any remains of a crater have long been worn away by snow and ice. On a clear day the dark pyramid-shaped peaks, and the white glaciers just below them, can be seen from a great distance in all directions.

Mount Kenya was revered by local people who believed it to be the home of Ngai, their God. The snow on the summit was a strange and apparently supernatural substance. The seemingly inexplicable presence of glaciers on an equatorial mountain also attracted the attention of European explorers. The first European to see Mount Kenya was the German missionary Ludwig Krapf who reached this part of Africa in 1849. His reports of a great mountain covered with snow were dismissed by European geographers until 1883, when it was also described by the young Scottish explorer Joseph Thomson.

Following these early reports, the first exploration of the mountain was led by the Austro-Hungarian Count Samuel Teleki in 1887. His expedition reached the snowline below the main peaks before being forced to turn back by rain and cold. The first truly scientific expedition to this part of East Africa was led by the British explorer Dr. J. W. Gregory, a geologist from the British Museum. His party reached Mount Kenya in 1893 and he applied names to many of the mountain's features including the Teleki Valley and the Lewis Glacier. Six years after that, in 1899, a party led by the Englishman Sir Halford Mackinder, reached the summit of Batian, at 5199m (17,054ft), the highest point on the mountain. Despite this attention Mount Kenya still remained obscure until 1929 when Eric Shipton, already an accomplished mountaineer, climbed to the summit of Nelion (5189m).

After the Second World War, Mount Kenya developed as a very popular area for walking and mountaineering. The Mountain Club of

Kenya (originally founded as the Mountain Club of East Africa in the 1930s) attracted many new members as climbing and mountain walking became more popular activities for Kenya's settlers and ex-patriate residents.

The mountain was originally named Mount Kenia by the Europeans, a corruption of one of its local names Kirenia, Kirinyaga, or Kima ya Kegnia (meaning Mountain of Whiteness or Mountain of the Ostrich, referring to the colour of the rocks and glaciers). The main peaks, Batian, Nelion and Lenana, were named by Mackinder after the Maasai chiefs Mbatiany, Neilieng and Olonana. At this time Kenya was called British East Africa and it was only later that the colony took its name from the mountain.

During colonial times, it was realized that the rainfall in the highlands surrounding Mount Kenya and the Aberdare Range was reliable, and the soil very fertile. Settlers were given exclusive farming rights and the Central Highland region also became known as the White Highlands. The area is still farmed and supports a fairly dense rural population, scattered over the farmland or grouped into small centres and larger towns. After a day's hiking through the foothills, however, walkers will leave the farmland and its people behind and enter a mountain wilderness, passing through dense rain forest, bamboo and open moorland before reaching the glaciers and jagged rock towers that surround the main peak area.

Best time to visit
The central peak area of Mount Kenya can be reached at any time of the year, but the best time for walkers is during the dry seasons, December-February, June-September, when the approach routes are generally passable for vehicles and conditions for camping and walking on the mountain trails are more pleasant. The finest periods are usually late January, early February and August. This latter period tends to be slightly cooler.

Walkers should note, however, that the weather patterns on Mount Kenya are notoriously unpredictable, and even during 'dry' seasons rain can fall and the weather can be very unpleasant for periods of two to three days.

Special conditions
The forest region around Mount Kenya is a designated forest reserve, and the area beyond this, mostly above the 3400m contour line, is gazetted as a national park. On the Chogoria Route, an extra nominal fee to the local council is also payable.

Due to the extreme conditions on Mount Kenya, walkers are not officially allowed to enter the park alone for longer than a day. Individuals who want to spend more than one day on the mountain must hire a guide to accompany them. This rule is necessary; the seriousness of high-level walking on Mount Kenya should not be underestimated. Experienced walkers preferring to be alone can avoid difficulties by teaming up with other walkers to get through the gate, or by employing a certain degree of diplomacy.

Several huts have been built on Mount Kenya by the Mountain Club of Kenya. Some of these are for public use, while others are reserved exclusively for full members of the club (temporary members cannot use these huts). Details on the public huts are included in each route description. Booking vouchers must be obtained to use the huts; these are available (40/- ppn, 1990) from Let's Go Travel, Nairobi, or the Naro Moru River Lodge.

Warnings

Every year hundreds of walkers reach the summit of Point Lenana. For them this is the literal and figurative high point of their challenging, yet rewarding, walk on Mount Kenya. Remember, however, that the peak area of Mount Kenya is over 4000m above sea level and that most walkers are likely to be affected by the altitude. Do not overestimate your own ability and level of acclimatization. Read and appreciate the advice on altitude in the Keeping healthy section on p60. Do not try to hurry up to the peaks unless you are acclimatized. Do not feel you have to reach Point Lenana. If your time is limited it is far better to walk up to the Summit Circuit Route, or simply enjoy walking below the Circuit on the higher sections of the various routes. As well as the main routes fully described in this book, a great many 'minor' routes exist diverting away from the popular trails to lesser-known valleys and tarns, or up to some of the higher foothills. The essential thing always is to enjoy yourself and not turn a hike on Mount Kenya into some kind of rigorous army-style march where reaching Point Lenana becomes more important than the pleasure of the walking itself.

Some of the huts on Mount Kenya are inhabited by mice or rats and surrounding areas infested by the rodent-like rock hyrax. If you are using the mountain huts keep all food out of these animals' reach.

General approaches

The southern slopes of the Mount Kenya massif are about 120km to the north/north-east of Nairobi. Good tarred roads join Nairobi to Nyeri and Embu (the two main towns on either side of the mountain's southern edge) via Sagana, and continue to completely encircle the mountain via Nanyuki and Meru. The road through Murang'a is in bad condition (March 1990). Petrol is usually available in the main towns.

Frequent bus and shared taxi services run from Nairobi to Nyeri and on to Nayuki via Naro Moro, or to Embu and on to Meru via Chogoria. Access to all of the routes up Mount Kenya is straightforward using public transport. (More specific information about the approaches to each route is contained in the individual route descriptions.)

The number of walking routes up to the peak area are limited by the forest zone which completely encircles the mountain. Tracks or paths have to be cut through the forest and, although many tracks are indicated on the various maps of Mount Kenya, only three of these are regularly maintained and suitable for walkers to follow without a guide. These three main routes are described along with a selection of walks around the peak area.

The upper end of each of the routes that lead to the central peaks area are all joined by the Summit Circuit Route, which completely circles the main peak area between the altitudes of 4300 and 4800 metres.

It is possible to traverse the mountain completely using a section of the Mount Kenya Circuit to link two routes. For this it is generally more convenient to use public transport, to avoid a journey back round the mountain to collect your car. Alternatively, drop-off or pick-up vehicles to take you round the mountain can be arranged at one of the mountain lodges. For walkers traversing the mountain the main routes are also described for a descent.

In this chapter on Mount Kenya the end of a route is normally regarded as its junction with the Summit Circuit. Walking times are given to the end of the route and from this junction to Austrian Hut, the usual start point for walkers going to the summit of Point Lenana.

From Austrian Hut to the summit of Point Lenana is 45 minutes - 1 hour's walking. It is generally advisable to do this walk in the early morning or late evening. At these times the peaks are above cloud level making sunrises and sunsets very dramatic.

The routes

The main routes up Mount Kenya are outlined here to give a brief introduction to distances and conditions likely to be encountered.

The Naro Moru Route Traditionally the Naro Moru Route is the most popular and straightforward of all the walking routes up Mount Kenya. It is also the quickest route to Austrian Hut and Point Lenana, but this can be a disadvantage for some walkers as they gain height too quickly and suffer from altitude sickness. Due to its popularity, the path is well marked and easy to follow.

The route starts at the small town of Naro Moru, on the western side of the mountain, between the towns of Nyeri and Nanyuki, and joins the Summit Circuit just above Mackinder's Camp, at the head of the Teleki Valley. The Naro Moru River Lodge makes a good base at the start of the route, and there are two bunkhouses and a number of campsites on the way up.

From the start of the route to Mackinder's Camp is usually a three-day walk. It is possible to drive, or get a lift, as far as the Met Station roadhead, at just over 3000m, which cuts the walk to Mackinder's to just one day. From Mackinder's Camp to Austrian Hut (for Point Lenana) is 2 - 4 hours' walking.

The Sirimon Route On the northern side of Mount Kenya, the Sirimon Route escapes some of the mountain's rainfall and is usually drier than

Camp near Mackinder's *On the Chogoria Route*

the other routes. This route is more undulating, however, and tends to be fairly strenuous.

The route starts near the small town of Timau, between the larger towns of Nanyuki and Meru, and joins the Summit Circuit at either Kami Hut or Simba Col. There is no ideal base at the start of this route. The nearest accommodation and campsite is at the Nanyuki River Lodge, about 15km to the south-west. On the route are two large, well-developed, bunkhouses plus a number of campsites and smaller huts.

From the start of this route to Kami Hut, or the nearby Shipton's Camp, is a 2 - 4 day walk. It is possible to drive to the roadhead at Old Moses Camp (3250m), cutting the walking time to Kami or Shipton's Camp to 1 - 2 days. Walking to Austrian Hut (for Point Lenana) takes another day.

The Chogoria Route The Chogoria Route begins at the small town of Chogoria, on the eastern side of Mount Kenya, between the larger towns of Embu and Meru, and joins the Summit Circuit at Square Tarn, about one hour's walk from Austrian Hut.

Chogoria town has shops and basic hotels, making a suitable base, and there are huts and campsites along the route.

The approach to the park gate passes through a wide section of the forest zone. The 25km of well maintained dirt road is good for vehicles but long and uninteresting for walkers. Driving time for this part of the route is 1 - 2 hours and, although it can be done in one day, most walkers take two days to reach the park gate. From Chogoria town to Austrian Hut walkers should allow 4 - 5 days. It is possible to drive to the roadhead, at 3350m, and walk from there to Austrian Hut in two days.

Other routes on the mountain tend to be poorly maintained and very seldom used. These include:

The Burguret Route This route is an old mule trail which was unused for many years until it was reopened by Bantu Lodge (now Mountain Rock Lodge) in the mid-1980s. Mountain Rock Lodge now organize tours up the Sirimon Route, and the Burguret Route has once again become overgrown and difficult to follow.

The route begins at Mountain Rock Lodge itself (which makes an obvious base) and leads up to Two Tarn Hut on the Summit Circuit. No permanent huts exist on this route, but there are a number of suitable campsites.

From the start of the route to Two Tarn Hut is a 3 - 4 day walk. It is possible to drive to an indistinct roadhead, at the end of the plantation area (around 2800m), and then reach Two Tarn Hut in 1 - 2 days. From Two Tarn Hut to Austrian Hut is 3 - 4 hours' walking.

The Timau Route This route starts just north of Timau town, on the northern side of the mountain, and joins the Chogoria Route near Minto's Hut. Approach routes pass through private land and, although drivable, tend to be confusing. There are no signposts. Paths on the upper sections of the route are very difficult to follow.

The Kamweti Route This route starts near Kianyaga village, on the southern side of the mountain, about 10km from Embu. The lower section of this route is drivable, passing an old rest house and forest station, but the upper sections of the route are seldom used by walkers as the path is unclear in places and conditions often extremely difficult. The route joins the Summit Circuit near Tilman Peak between Mackinder's Camp and Austrian Hut.

The Old Moses Route This route starts near Naro Moru village and runs to the north of the Naro Moru Route to meet it near Mackinder's Camp. This route is seldom used and has virtually disappeared in many places.

Maps
SK 1:50M maps are very difficult to find as suppliers in Nairobi and at the OS in Britain are out of stock. The OS *Tourist Map and Guide of Mount Kenya*, and the *Mount Kenya Map and Guide* published by A. Wielochowski, are both widely available. Details in the Maps section on p55.

The Naro Moru Route

Approach
The good quality tar road that circles Mount Kenya runs along the

western side of the massif, linking the large towns of Nyeri and Nanyuki, passing through the small town of Naro Moru, 25km south of Nanyuki, 35km north of Nyeri. Cars can be safely left in Naro Moru at the Naro Moru River Lodge, at the Mount Kenya Youth Hostel or at the Met Station roadhead. Petrol is usually available in Naro Moru town, and also at Nanyuki and Nyeri.

Naro Moru River Lodge operate a daily transfer bus to and from Nairobi. Public transport (bus, matatu, shared taxi) along the Nyeri - Nanyuki road, via Naro Moru town, is frequent.

The lodge is about 2km from the town; around 30/- for you and your equipment, if required, in a local taxi or van. A local matatu service runs along the Mount Kenya road past the youth hostel (10km from Naro Moru town).

Naro Moru has a market, some shops and a simple lodging house.

Accommodation and services
Naro Moru River Lodge is a country hotel, set in pleasant gardens, offering hotel accommodation (d 1580/- hb, 1760/- fb, 1990) and self-catering cottages (920/- for 2 to 2050/- for 7, 1990). A bunkhouse (120/-) and campsite (40/-) are also available. The hotel has a restaurant (dinner 250/-) and a bar full of Mount Kenya maps and mementos. Other facilities include swimming, tennis, squash and horse-riding. The lodge's Mountain Office deals with all aspects of walking and climbing on Mount Kenya. Services and charges are as follows: transport to the roadhead, 600/- for the vehicle (plus park fees, 65/-); guides 90/-, cook 90/-, porters 80/- per day (porter payload 16kg for a 3 day safari); equipment can be hired and reservations made for the bunkhouses at the Met Station (140/-) and Teleki Lodge/Mackinder's Camp (230/-). These two permanent camps are leased from the park and administered by the lodge. The Mountain Office staff also offer a consultation service providing detailed information about all aspects of the routes, conditions and equipment required on Mount Kenya (100/-). Luggage can be stored at the lodge for 20/- per day. For inquiries and reservations contact Let's Go Travel, Nairobi, or the lodge's Nairobi office: Alliance Hotels, College House, corner of Koinange Street and University Way, PO Box 49839, Nairobi, Tel 337501, 20149.

The Mount Kenya Youth Hostel, reopened in 1989 after a fire destroyed the original building, has bandas, a campsite (s 40/, c 25/-, 1990), clean water, toilets and showers. There is a small local-style snack bar on the site and dukas nearby. Porters and guides can be arranged.

Mountain Rock Lodge, also called Bantu Lodge, 8km north of Naro Moru. The lodge is 1km to the east of the main road but the entrance gate is clearly marked by a large painting of Mount Kenya on the fence. Accommodation is in cottages (s 260/-, d 550 bb, 1070/- fb, 1990) and there is a campsite (50/-). The lodge has a restaurant (dinner 140/-) and

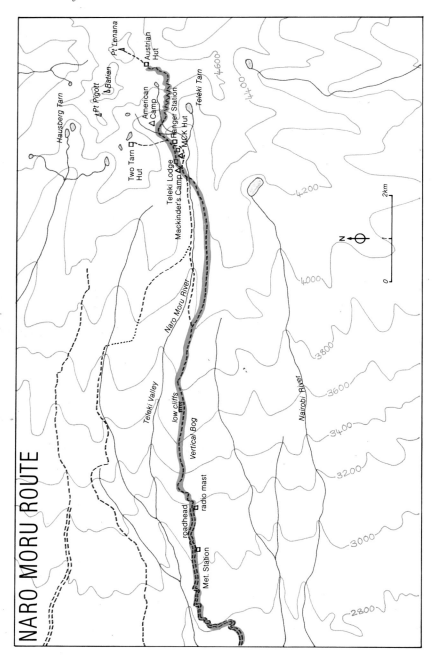

NARO MORU ROUTE

bar. Mountain Rock Lodge operates various organized walking tours, mainly on the Sirimon Route. Services and charges are as follows: transport to roadhead 1200/- per vehicle, return; guides 95/-, porters 85/- per day. Reservations and payments can be made here for the two bunkhouses on the Sirimon Route, Old Moses Camp (200/-) and Shipton's Camp (250/-), that are leased from the park and administered by Mountain Rock Lodge. No equipment is available for hire. Shorter one-day walks are also offered in the forest near the lodge for bird-watching, or visiting the Burguret Waterfalls and the Mau Mau Caves, a hidden 'conference centre' for freedom fighters during the Emergency. For information and reservations contact the lodge direct: PO Box 333, Nanyuki Tel (01772) 2098/9, or their agents in Nairobi: Aardvark Safaris, IPS Buildings, Kimathi Street; or Special Camping Safaris, Gilfillan House, Kenyatta Avenue, Tel 338325, 20072.

Naro Moru Town to Met Station

[1]		From the **crossroads [1]** on the main tar road in Naro Moru town, a good dirt road leads east towards the mountain past huts and fields (national park signposted). After 3km fork right and after a farther 3km turn left, passing the youth hostel and a small village. At the next junction, fork left past a small road camp and a sign warning heavy vehicles that the road is closed in the wet, to cross a wooden bridge and enter the pine forest.
5-8 hrs	18 km	
[2]		The road forks at a junction marked by a stone model of Mount Kenya: left to Gathiuru Forest Station; right past the airfield to reach the **park gate [2]**, the park sub-HQ and the workers' village. Entrance fees must be paid at the gate. There is a campsite on a grassy area amongst trees just beyond the gate and a small shop selling a few basic items.
[3]		
2½-4 hrs	7 km	From the **park gate [3]** the drivable track continues to climb through the forest, steep and rough in places, to reach the public roadhead and the **Met Station [4]** campsite and bunkhouses (3050m).
[4]		

From Naro Moru town to the Met Station is 25km. Fit walkers can cover this in a day, but are advised to find a lift at least part way or break the journey at the park gate. Drivers should allow 1^1/$_2$ - 2 hours, allowing time for formalities at the gate.

(1) Naro Moro to Yoth hostel (walk/lift) 10km
(2) through metstation gate to Met station 16km
(3) Mackinder' Camp -

Met Station to Mackinder's Camp and Teleki Lodge
4 - 6 hours 1150m (4) Austran hut : (5) Summit + down (6) leave -

[1]
0.25
[2]
0.15
[3]
I
0.35
I
[4]
0.30
[5]
I
I
1.00
I
I
[6]
I
0.45
I
[7]
.
0.25
.
[8]
0.10
[9]

From the **Met Station [1]** follow the drivable track (official vehicles only) up to the **radio station [2]**. The track becomes a clear path and continues to climb up through forest before suddenly breaking out into open **heathland [3]**. If the weather is clear the entire Aberdare Range can be seen to the west on the other side of the wide flat Nyeri Valley. The first of the red and white marker posts is reached indicating the route through the steep boggy section known as the vertical bog. After dry periods, however, this section is not difficult.

The gradient eases and walkers get their **first view [4]** of the main peaks since entering the forest. The path continues to gain height keeping mainly to a small rock ridge. At one point the path passes below and to the right of a series of **low cliffs [5]** offering shelter from sun, wind and (to a lesser extent) rain. This makes a good resting place, as the amount of picnic litter shows.

The path continues to climb, still following the marker posts, until a **fork [6]** is reached at a vantage point overlooking the Teleki Valley. The left path drops steeply to the Naro Moru River then follows the river upstream on its northern bank. The path to the right drops much more gradually to **cross the river [7]** at a point about 3km further upstream.

After the paths have converged, continue to aim up towards the head of the valley, past signposts indicating **Mackinder's Camp [8]** (the campsite) and up a short rocky spur to reach **Teleki Lodge [9]** (the bunkhouse) at 4200m.

The bunkhouse has dormitories and a communal area for cooking and eating. Water is piped down from a stream. Camping is permitted outside the lodge, at Mackinder's Camp, or at any point in the Teleki Valley between the Met Station and Teleki Lodge (15/-).

Beyond Teleki Lodge, about 0.5km or 10 minutes' walk farther up the valley, is the Mountain Club of Kenya hut, locked and reserved strictly for MCK members only, and the ranger station, permanently manned and in radio contact with the park HQ.

From Teleki Lodge
Walkers are recommended to spend two nights at Mackinder's Camp/Teleki Lodge to acclimatize more effectively. A number of interesting day-excursions are possible:

Teleki Tarn From Teleki Lodge, Shipton's Peak, with a pointed summit and steep west face, is clearly visible at the head of the valley. To the right of the peak is a large corrie, a bowl-shaped depression. Teleki Tarn is at the base of this corrie. Follow the path from Teleki Lodge down onto the valley floor passing below and to the right of the MCK hut and the ranger station. Cross some small streams and a boggy section aiming for the lowest point in the U-shaped lip at the open side of the corrie. A waterfall flows over the left side of the lip and the path goes up a small scree slope to the right of the waterfall to the edge of the lip then drops to reach the tarn. (1 - 2 hours there and back.)

American Camp From Teleki Lodge take the path along the left (north) side of the valley passing above and to the left of the MCK hut and ranger station. Keep high and fork left at a junction aiming directly towards the main peaks. Follow occasional cairns through groundsels and around large boulders, across a stream and over a small knoll to reach the flat area at the northern head of the Teleki Valley called American Camp. This is an excellent campsite with fine views of the Darwin and Diamond Glaciers, the Gate of the Mists between the twin summits of Nelion and Batian. (30 - 45 minutes from Teleki Lodge.)

From American Camp a good walk is up the scree to Hut Tarn, Two Tarn Hut and Arthur's Seat. Full details in the Summit Circuit Route description.

Another interesting short walk from American Camp is up to the foot, or snout, of the Tyndal Glacier, visible between Point Pigott and Batian. Cairns mark a path up to the lip of the moraine but this is only slightly easier than scrambling over large boulders from American Camp straight up to the lowest point on the lip to reach the tarn. Pass the tarn either to the left or right and continue scrambling up to the foot of the glacier. (45 mins - 1 hour up from American Camp, 1 hour down to Teleki Lodge.)

Teleki Lodge and Mackinder's Camp to Austrian Hut and Point Lenana
2 - 3 hours 590m

[1] 0.10 **[2]** 0.15 **[3]** 1.00 **[4]** 0.45 **[5]**	From the **lodge [1]** take the path along the left (north) side of the valley, passing above and to the left of the MCK hut and **ranger station [2]**. At a junction fork right and trend right across the head of the valley. To the left of Shipton's Peak is a very large scree slope; the path can be seen zig-zagging up this. Reach the **foot [3]** of the scree and keep to the right side of the slope as it climbs and trends gradually left. The path reaches the **crest [4]** of a small ridge from where the huge expanse of the Lewis Glacier can be clearly and dramatically seen. Beyond the glacier is the imposing south-east face of Nelion, spectacular if seen in the early morning light. The gradient eases slightly as the path trends left (north-east) across a small rocky plateau then climbs again on loose rocks and scree to reach **Austrian Hut [5]** and Top Hut (4790m). From Austrian Hut the summit of Point Lenana is clearly

visible to the right of the Lewis Glacier. The path aims straight for the summit. Keep to rock where possible and avoid loose scree, snow and ice to reach the **summit [6]** (4985m) in 45 minutes - $1^1/_2$ hours.

From the summit it is possible to see back to Austrian and Top Huts and down to the head of the Teleki Valley. Across the Lewis and Gregory Glaciers are Point Thomson and the two main summits of Nelion and Batian (partially obscured). Farther to the right (north-west) Mackinder's Valley (with the Sirimon Route) can be seen, and continuing right (north-east) the Gorges Valley (with the Chogoria Route), Hall Tarns and the precipice of The Temple are clearly visible. On clear mornings the peaks of Kilimanjaro and Mawenzi, over 350km away to the south, can be seen above the clouds. The views from Point Lenana are usually good in the morning and particularly spectacular at sunrise, although care should be taken when ascending in the dark. From Point Lenana back down to Austrian Hut takes about 25 minutes.

Austrian Hut has room for 30 people to sleep comfortably. Sleeping platforms and cooking benches are provided and all doors and windows are in place. Other facilities are spartan; the single pit toilet is often full and water must be carried from the Curling Pond (after breaking the ice) 200m away. Payments to use Austrian Hut (40/-) can be made at Naro Moru River Lodge or at Let's Go Travel, Nairobi. Top Hut, next to Austrian Hut, is officially for MCK members only, but in recent years it seems to have been abandoned and is now used mainly by porters. Camping is also possible near Austrian Hut, but tent pegs are difficult to get in; bring plenty of cord and tie your tent down with rocks.

The Sirimon Route

Approach
The good quality tar road that circles Mount Kenya runs round the northern edge of the massif linking the large towns of Nanyuki and Meru, passing through the small town of Timau. For drivers, Timau is 20km to the north-east of Nanyuki and 60km west of Meru. Coming from

The People Who Know Camping SAFARI SEEKERS

Room 544, 5th Floor, Jubilee Insurance Exchange, Kaunda Street
P.O. Box 9165, Nairobi, Kenya. Tel: 26206 Fax: 334585

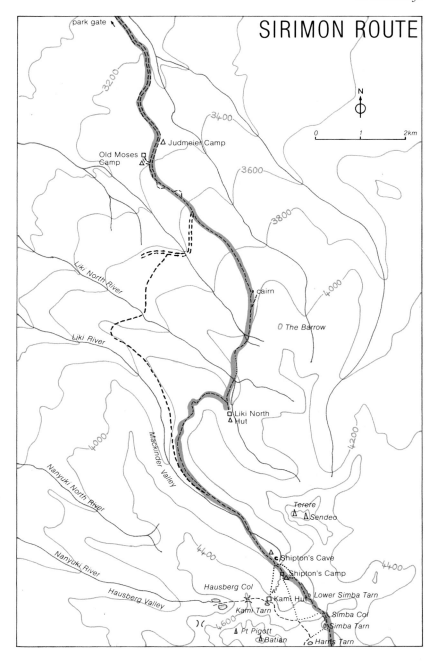

SIRIMON ROUTE

park gate

3200

N

3400

0 1 2km

△ Judmeier Camp

Old Moses □
Camp △

3600

3800

Liki North River

cairn

4000

Liki River

□ The Barrow

□ Liki North
△ Hut

Mackinder Valley

4000

4200

Nanyuki North River

Terere
△ △ Sendeo

Nanyuki River

4400

△
c Shipton's Cave

□ Shipton's Camp
△

Hausberg Col

Hausberg Valley

□ Lower Simba Tarn

□ Kami Hut

Kami Tarn

Simba Col

4600

Simba Tarn

△ Pt Pigott

△ Batian

Harris Tarn

4400

Nanyuki, the dirt track to the Sirimon Gate is signposted on the right (south) side of the main road about 5km before Timau, and 1km before a large concrete bridge that carries the main road over the Sirimon River. There is no suitable place to leave vehicles at the start of the route, but cars can be left at the park gate or at Old Moses Camp (the roadhead). Petrol supplies at Timau are unreliable, but generally available at Nanyuki and Meru.

Public transport (buses, matatus and shared taxis) along the Nanyuki - Meru road is frequent, but there is no service up to the park gate.

Naro Moru River Lodge and Mountain Rock (Bantu) Lodge both offer organized walking tours on the Sirimon Route and have their own transport for taking walkers to either the park gate or the roadhead. Nanyuki River Lodge does not offer organized tours but can help to arrange porters, guides and transfers.

There is no settlement at the start of the Sirimon Route to make a suitable base for walkers. Timau is small with only a few local stores, although Nanyuki has a market and shops with a wider selection of goods. The Nanyuki River Lodge, on the north-east side of the town, has rooms (d 500/-, 1990) and a campsite (40/-). Other suggested bases are Naro Moru River Lodge and Mountain Rock (Bantu) Lodge (details in Naro Moru Route section on p84).

Main road - Sirimon Gate

The Sirimon Gate (2650m) is 9km from the main road along a well-signposted dirt track. The track splits at three junctions; take the left fork at each. After 5km pass a sign marking the park boundary. Cars with two-wheel drive can reach the gate except in very wet conditions. All park fees must be paid at the gate. Camping is permitted on a grassy site, with water and a pit toilet, nearby.

Sirimon Gate to Old Moses Camp
3 - 5 hours 700m

From the **gate [1]** follow the drivable track through forest which prevents clear views of the main peaks. After a steep and rocky section the track levels out around a right-hand bend. On the left is a **grassy clearing [2]** suitable for camping. Water is available from a stream 200m down to the left.

Continue through the forest. After a steep section the gradient eases and the forest begins to thin out. The main peak area is clearly visible as the path passes through **heathland [3]**. The green roof of Old Moses Camp can be seen behind a small knoll.

Once again a flat section is followed by a steep rocky section. On the left, just before an unmanned barrier, is **Judmeier**

Camp **[4]** (3340m), a grassy campsite with a large fireplace and pit toilet. Water is available from the stream by the track just beyond the barrier.

Old Moses Camp [5] (3350m) is built on a knoll to the right of the main track half a kilometre, or ten minutes' walk, from Judmeier Camp.

Old Moses Camp is administered by Mountain Rock Lodge. A bed in the bunkhouse can be paid for in advance, or to the caretaker on arrival (100/-). Camping is also possible here (20/-). To reach Old Moses Camp vehicles usually require four-wheel drive.

The fit and acclimatized can walk from Old Moses Camp to Shipton's Camp in one day, and then reach Austrian Hut or Point Lenana on the next. To help acclimatization, however, walkers may prefer to break the journey at Liki North Hut or stay two nights at Shipton's Camp from where a number of interesting day-excursions can be made.

Old Moses Camp to Liki North Hut
3 - 4 hours 640m

From **Old Moses Camp [1]** rejoin the main track and follow it, aiming south and south-easterly, up a broad ridge between two river valleys aiming towards the prominent long rounded hill called The Barrow. About 30 minutes' walking from Old Moses Camp, the drivable track divides; keep right. The track crosses a **small stream [2]** and a faint grassy track branches off to the right; keep straight on on the 'main' track. The track divides again (but the branches converge again within 1km) then peters out into a grassy path which continues to aim for The Barrow. At a cairn on a **lone boulder [3]** the path veers rightwards (south) towards the main peaks, following cairns round the head of a valley crossing several boggy streams and then climbing to reach a **ridge crest [4]** marked by a red and white marker post. The path becomes indistinct as it drops to a stream in the valley bottom. Reach the stream and follow it upstream on the right side (past another marker post) to reach **Liki North Hut [5]** (3990m).

The hut is small (sleeps 8) and poorly maintained but in a fine position, next to the stream on the floor of the valley that drops down from the Terere and Sendeo Peaks. Upstream 75m is a good camping place.

Liki North Hut to Shipton's Camp
3 - 4 hours 250m

From the **hut [1]** follow the clear path (marker posts and cairns) as it climbs up to a **ridge top [2]** and drops down in to the Mackinder Valley (cairns) to reach a single **marker post [3]** just before crossing a small pebbly stream. Follow the path as it climbs gradually, trending towards the river to **cross it [4]** and the continue up the right (south) bank. The path passes steeply to the right of a series of overhangs **(Shipton's Caves) [5]** to reach flatter ground. An indistinct path braches off left across to the east side of the valley floor (eventually to Lower Simba Tarn and Simba Col; keep straight on to reach **Shipton's Camp [6]** (4240m) which is visible on a knoll ahead.

The Shipton's Camp bunkhouse (administered by Mountain Rock Lodge, and also called Shipton's Cave Camp) sleeps about thirty people. Camping is on a grassy area nearby (20/-). Water from stream.

Old Moses Camp to Shipton's Camp (Direct)

This alternative route is longer, but less undualting than the route via Liki North Hut, and involves less walking time (5 -7 hours). However, it tends to be more boggy, and does not afford the spectacular views of the main peaks that are visible from points on the route via Liki North Hut. It is therefore recommended only as a descent route.

From Shipton's Camp

Most walkers aiming for Point Lenana walk to Austrian Hut around the eastern side of the mountain via Simba Col and Tooth Col. It is also possible to approach Point Lenana from Shipton's Camp directly, via Harris Tarn, although this route involves some steep and intimidating scrambling.

For walkers staying two nights at Shipton's Camp to acclimatize, possible destinations for an easy day-hike include:

Lower Simba Tarn: Walkers planning to approach Point Lenana directly via Harris Tarn, or approach Austrian Hut via the southern section of the Summit Circuit, will otherwise miss this picturesque spot which makes an easy rest-day destination. Even those who intend to walk via Lower Simba Tarn on their way to Austrian Hut could walk this far on the preceding day to check the route as the path crosses stony ground and is indistinct in places. Directions opposite (1 - 1^1/2 hours, there and back).

Hausberg Col: Follow the steep path up to Kami Huts visible up on the valley side to south-west of Shipton's Camp, then continue climbing eastwards up yellow scree to the lowest point on the ridge to the right (north) of Point Peter and the main peaks. Excellent views north-east over the head of Mackinder's valley, west down Hausberg Valley and of the northern face of the main peak area (1 - $1^1/2$ hours up, 30 mins down).

Hausberg Tarn and Oblong Tarn: From Hausberg Col the path zig-zags west and down to tarns which make a good lunch stop. Good views of Point Peter, the Joseph and Cesar Glaciers, Arthur's Seat and the Western Terminal. From Shipton's Camp to Hausberg and Oblong Tarns is $2^1/2$ - 4 hours' walking, there and back. (Full details in the Summit Circuit Route description.)

From Shipton's Camp to Austrian Hut, via Simba Col (i.e. the 'usual' route) is 3 - 4 hours' walking (height again 550m), but two alternative routes are available.

Shipton's Camp to Square Tarn via Simba Col

[1] 0.30 **[2]** 1.15 **[3]** 0.02 **[4]** 0.20 **[5]**	From **Shipton's Camp [1]** aim east, around the left side of the rocky bluff in front (south) of the camp, to meet the path to Lower Simba Tarn which runs along the southern bank of the stream (and occasional cairns) up to reach **Lower Simba Tarn [2]**. From the south-eastern end of the tarn aim south-east up the left side of a bouldery scree slope. Trend leftwards to skirt around a rocky buttress on its left side then aim straight up towards the lowest point on the skyline, **Simba Col [3]**. From Simba Col drop down a short scree slope **(Upper) Simba Tarn [4]**, which is passed on its left (east) side, and continue to trend right and gradually upwards (following cairns) across boulders to cross another ridge and drop to **Square Tarn [5]**.

Shipton's Camp to Square Tarn via Harris Tarn

[1] 1.15 **[2]** 0.10	The rocky bluff directly in front (south) of **Shipton's Camp [1]** is split by a broad, steep, stone-filled gulley, with a large cairn at its base. Scramble up this gulley, between a rocky gap at the top, to cross easier ground (marked by cairns) to reach the foot of a large steep scree-slope. A zig-zag path can be seen climbing the scree-slope aiming directly towards the summit of Point Lenana, and a point on the ridge to the right (south-east) and higher than Simba Col. Follow this path (cairns) to reach **Harris Tarn [2]**. Pass to the left of Harris Tarn then contour round to the right across steep rocky ground. The path is indistinct but occasional cairns mark the way. Maintain height where

Point Lenana from Harris Tarn   *Chogoria Route: The Temple*

possible to reach a **small col [3]**. Point Lenana is up to the right. Drop down, trending left, into the small rocky valley between two spurs extending from Lenana to reach **Square Tarn [4]**.

Square Tarn to Austrian Hut via Tooth Col

To the south of **Square Tarn [1]** a prominent ridge extends north-west to south-east linking Point Lenana to Coryndon and Delamere Peaks. A number of buttresses and pinnacles stand along the edge of this ridge. About 200m to the left (south-east) of the lowest point on this ridge is a sharp, roughly triangular, pinnacle; The Tooth. The lowest point on the ridge is Tooth Col and the path towards Austrian Hut passes through here.

Various paths lead up the rocky scree from Square Tarn to **Tooth Col [2]**. From Tooth Col drop down and trend right across the Hobley Valley (with excellent views to the south and south-east of Hanging Tarn below the west face of Coryndon Peak and Thompson's Tarns on the valley floor). Follow this path up to the crest of the major ridge to reach **Austrian Hut [3]** (4790m). (The silhouette of the toilet at Austrian Hut can be seen on the lowest point of the sky-line!)

Harris Tarn to Point Lenana

The summit of Point Lenana is clearly visible from Harris Tarn. Down the ridge to the right (north) of the summit are two rock needles. (If weather conditions obscure the peak, do not attempt this route.) It is possible to scramble fairly comfortably up this path, although it is steep and intimidating in places. If you start using your hands for more than balance and the occasional helpful pull you are off-route.

From the eastern end of **Harris Tarn [1]** the path climbs up small scree then trends left and up to loose boulders. From here occasional cairns mark the way as it zig-zags steeply up to a point on the ridge, where the gradient is less steep, between the needles and the actual summit (see photo). At the ridge, turn left to reach the summit of **Point Lenana [2]**.

Austrian Hut is clearly visible from the summit and can be reached easily by following the path down the rocky ridge (about 25 minutes).

Chogoria Route

Approach

The good quality tar road that circles Mount Kenya runs round the eastern side of the massif linking the large towns of Embu and Meru. The small town of Chogoria is signposted just to the west of this main road, 75km north of Embu and 55km south of Meru. Arrangements could be made in Chogoria to leave a vehicle but cars can be left at the park gate or the roadhead and this is more usual. Petrol is not always available in Chogoria but supplies at Meru and Embu are reliable.

Public transport along the Meru - Embu road is frequent, but there is no service up to the park gate.

Chogoria town has a market and a number of shops selling basic supplies, although special items should be brought from Nairobi.

For accommodation the Chogoria Guest House, on the right side of the short main street (s 60/-, d 120/-, c 10/-, 1990), and the Chogoria Transit Motel, about 2km south of Chogoria centre (d 120/-), are both used to visiting walkers and can help to arrange guides, porters and transport to the park gate, if required. Walkers preferring not to stay can still make arrangements through either of these hotels.

Chogoria has three porters and guides associations but rates are standardized: guides charge 130/- per day, porters 120/-. Cost of hiring a four-wheel drive vehicle to the park gate is 800/- to 1200/- (1990), depending on track conditions.

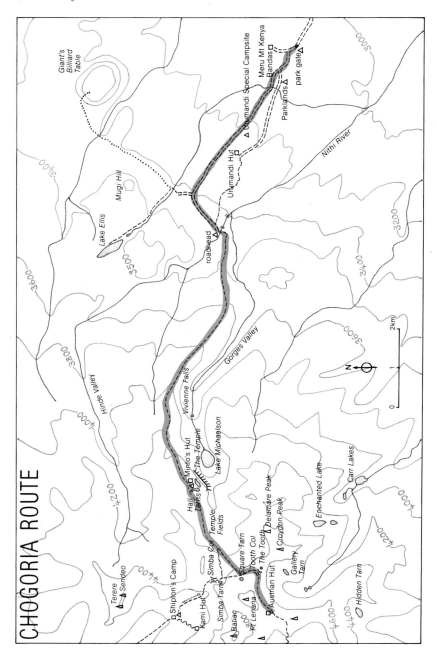

CHOGORIA ROUTE

Chogoria Town to Forest Station

The Chogoria Park Gate is 25km from Chogoria town along a dirt track which is generally well maintained but can be impassable after heavy rain. From the end of the tar road follow the main dirt track and follow the main track as it forks left after 1km. At the next junction fork right (signposted Chogoria Forest Station), over a small bridge, past the Chogoria Guides and Porters sign, over a large bridge, fork right (signposted Mount Kenya National Park, Chogoria Gate) and fork right again to reach the Chogoria Forest Station.

All visitors must stop at the forest gate and sign a register. Camping is sometimes permitted at the forest station.

Forest Station to Park Gate

The drivable track leads from the forest station through dense forest for 22km to the Chogoria Park Gate. It is possible for walkers to break this section by camping at Bairunyi Clearing, 14km from the forest gate, but water is hard to find here so it is best to walk this section in one stretch if possible to avoid carrying water. For drivers the final 5km of the track before the park gate is steep and rocky, so a vehicle with four-wheel drive is recommended.

All entrance fees must be paid at the park gate. Beyond the gate, fork right to reach the Meru Mount Kenya Bandas; self-catering accommodation for up to 16 people (s 240/-, 1990). (For reservations and information contact Let's Go Travel in Nairobi.) Fork left, then left again for the public campsite, in an area sometimes referred to as Parklands, about 300m from the park gate. This grassy site has water, toilets and a shelter. The daily park charge covers camping here but the site is owned and maintained by the county council who make a nominal additional charge.

The park gate is at 3020m. From Chogoria Forest Station to Chogoria Park Gate takes about 1 hour driving, 6 - 8 hours' walking.

Park Gate to The Roadhead
2 - 3 hours 280m

[1]
0.30
[2]
1.15
[3]
0.30
[4]

Rejoin the main vehicle track from the **bandas** or **campsite [1]** and follow this north-westerly. Cross a small river, and pass a **sign [2]** indicating Urumandi Special Campsite (to left). The track continues through glade country, climbing steeply in a number of places. At a **small cairn [3]** the track forks: right to Lake Ellis and the Giant's Billiards Table; left to reach the **roadhead [4]** (3300m).

An alternative route for walkers passes to the south of the main track via Urumandi Hut to rejoin at the roadhead.

Camping is possible at the roadhead (water from the stream, no other facilities) and cars can be left.

From the roadhead
To help acclimatization walkers may prefer to spend two nights at the roadhead, or one at the park gate and the next at the roadhead (especially if the section from the forest station has been covered in one day). If so, a number of interesting day-excursions can be made:

Lake Ellis From the roadhead, retrace to the cairn, turn left and follow the drivable track down until it turns into a path (turning space) that continues down to cross two small streams then forks left (cairn). (The right fork contours round the hillside towards the Giant's Billiards Table.) The path climbs uphill, through tussock grass and heather, to reach a small flat spot at the convergence of three small valleys with a small rock outcrop visible ahead. Continue to gain height, keeping the outcrop on your left (occasional cairns). Pass a small stagnant tarn on its left side and continue to reach the south-east tip of Lake Ellis. A number of spots around the lake make ideal campsites (2 - 3 hours' walking, there and back).

Giant's Billiards Table This large flat-topped hill is visible from many points along the Chogoria Route including the Parklands campsite and the summit of Lenana. Follow the directions above and fork right at the cairn where the left path leads to Lake Ellis. The path is indistinct in places, but the Billiards Table itself is clearly visible as a landmark. Contour round the right (east) side of Mugi Hill then drop into a valley to cross a stream. The easiest way up to the top of the Billiards Table is to walk around the base to the north side, which is lower, then scramble up to the circular plateau which can be crossed to its western edge for the best views of Mugi Hill and the main peaks of Mount Kenya in the distance (3 - 4 hours' walking, there and back).

Roadhead to Minto's Hut
4 - 6 hours 1000m

[1]
1.00
[2]

1.45

[3]

The path from the **roadhead [1]** drops slightly to cross a stream then begins to climb up a ridge, steeply in places. At a **definite flattening [2]** of the ridge the main peaks come into view. The path continues to climb in steps of alternately steep and easy gradients, with spectacular views up to the main peaks and down into the gorge with the Nithi River, the Vivienne Falls and Lake Michelson all visible. Behind (east) Lake Ellis and the Billiards Table can also be clearly seen. To the left is a 100m high detached rock **pinnacle [3]**. The ridge becomes broader with small outcrops and scattered

I
0.40
.
[4]
.
0.10
[5]
.
0.05
.
[6]
I
0.40
I
[7]

boulders as the path contours around the left side of the ridge about 30m below the crest to reach the base of an **obvious col [4]**. Continue to gain height, then contour round the head of a **hanging corrie [5]** (a large bowl-shaped depression some 500m across) to cross a **small stream [6]**, with a crude rock shelter nearby, and pass below and to the left of a large perched block (10m high).

Follow the path as it crosses the corrie floor and starts to climb steeply up the rocky hillside, to the right of where the corrie falls away into the main gorge. Cross numerous lava bowls (small plateaux between rocky knolls) to reach Hall Tarns and **Minto's Hut [7]** (4300m).

Minto's is a square corrugated iron hut with cooking benches and sleeping platforms for 16 people. The hut belongs to the Mountain Club of Kenya and visitors are officially required to pay a fee to use it (40/-). There is no caretaker, but visiting rangers or MCK officials may check for booking vouchers. Near the hut, around the tarns, are several idyllic camping places. Water is available from the tarns, but there is no reliable water source between the roadhead and Minto's.

Five minutes' walk to the south from Minto's is The Temple, the top of the Gorges Valley where the walls of the gorge are at their highest, steepest and most impressive. This high vantage point affords a spectacular view over the upper reaches of the Nithi River and Lake Michelson.

Minto's Hut to Austrian Hut
$2^1/2$ - 4 hours 490m

[1]
I
0.40
I
[2]
I
I
I
I
I
I
I
I
[3]
I

The path winds around the north side of the **large tarn [1]** then aims up the valley directly towards Point Lenana, visible to the left of the main peaks. The gradient is easy and the path clear to the **head of the valley [2]**. Below and to the left is a broad, flat, grassy area surrounded on three sides by steep scree slopes. This area, sometimes called **Temple Fields [2]**, is good for camping.

Point Lenana, with its flat-topped summit, dominates the view to the south-west. Batian and Nelion are behind and to the right of Lenana. To the left (south-east) of Lenana a ridge with numerous buttresses and pinnacles of various shapes and sizes forms the skyline. To the left of the lowest point of this ridge is a sharp, roughly triangular, pinnacle; The Tooth. The path to Austrian Hut passes through this lowest point; Tooth Col.

Trend right, above and to the right of **Temple Fields [3]**, and begin to climb steeply across rocks and scree. The **path divides**

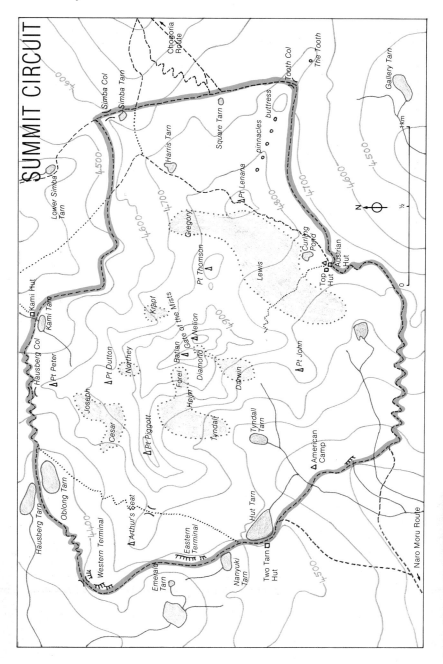

0.05

[4]

|

0.30

|

[5]

0.05

[6]

|

0.20

|

[7]

[4]: the right path keeps to the floor of the broad rocky valley, then climbs up a narrow scree gulley to the left of a series of low grey cliffs, to reach (Upper) Simba Tarn and Simba Col; the left path trends leftwards up the steep scree, then turns sharply left to zig-zag up the steepest section of the slope. Lenana and the main peaks are hidden from view.

Continue to climb steeply until a **flat section [5]** is reached and Point Lenana becomes visible again up to the right. Tooth Col is visible straight ahead (šouth). Cross the boulder plain (cairns), and pass above and to the left of **Square Tarn [6]**, in a depression 200m to right, up bouldery scree to **Tooth Col [7]**. For directions from Tooth Col to Austrian Hut see the end of the Sirimon Route description.

The Summit Circuit Route

A full circuit of the main peaks area involves 5 - 8 hours' walking which can be completed in one or two days and followed in either direction. Fit and acclimatized walkers, travelling light with a dawn start, can return to their starting point before the midday mists arrive. Walkers with the time available may prefer a less hurried approach and split the journey by camping (or staying in a hut) half-way round. Although the path is cairned it can be difficult to follow when reference points, such as cols or peaks, are obscured by mist.

Walkers traversing the mountain will need to follow some sections of the Summit Circuit to link their ascent and descent routes.

If a complete circuit is not possible some sections of the route can be covered by walkers on an out and back basis, and as there are a number of

Tooth Col and The Tooth: Viewed from Austrian Hut

places on the Summit Circuit where alternative paths are available, certain sections of this route can be covered without having to backtrack completely.

Summit Circuit Route - Anti-clockwise

Austrian Hut to Kami huts
2 – 3 hours

[1]

0.25

[2]

0.10

[3]

0.25

[4]

1.10

[5]

From **Austrian Hut [1]** aim south-east (with your back to the south-east face of Nelion) for 50m to the lip of the col that overlooks the head of the Hobley Valley, then trend left (north-east) following a clearly cairned path round the head of the valley, across bouldery scree, passing below and to the right of Point Lenana, a ridge crest (with five minor stunted pinnacles) and a large buttress (100m high, red with black streaks) before trending left and more steeply upwards to reach **Tooth Col [2]** (200m to the left of a prominent triangular buttress; The Tooth (see photo p102). From Tooth Col it is possible to see down into the Gorges Valley (with the Chogoria Route); Hall Tarns, on a terrace above the sheer rock cliffs of the Temple, are clearly visible.

The path drops down scree to **Square Tarn [3]** and divides. Take the path leading straight on (the path to the right drops down into the Gorges Valley and connects with the Chogoria Route), over a small col and continue to follow cairns, trending left and down towards **Simba Tarn [4]**. Another path leads eastwards from here, also connecting with the Chogoria Route, but aim north-west over Simba Col (a low point in the ridge that extends north-east from Point Lenana).

From Simba Col it is possible to see down into the Mackinder Valley (with the Sirimon Route). The path leads into the valley then divides : the right path drops steeply down towards Lower Simba Tarn and Shipton's Camp; take the left path (indistinct) which contours across large scree slopes to meet another path coming straight down from Harris Tarn.

Continue down to another fork marked by a large cairn: take the left path (the path striaght on leads down to Shipton's Camp) to continue contouring over scree slopes, then a large bouldery area at the foot of high steep cliffs, to reach **Kami Huts [5]** (4425m) on a flat area on the left (west) side of the valley.

Alternatively, from Simba Col follow the path which climbs steeply parallel and to the left (south-east) of ridge (which leads eventually to

Point Lenana) to reach the right (north) side of Harris Tarn. From here a cairned path aims steeply down the scree towards Shipton's Camp. Take this path down to the fork marked by a large cairn described in the previous paragraph, then follow the same descriptions to reach Kami Huts.

Camping is possible by Kami Tarn, For details see the Sirimon Route description.

Kami Huts to Tarn Hut
2 – 3^1/$_2$ hours

---

[1]

0.20

[2]

0.20

[3]
[4]

0.30

[5]
0.10

[6]

From **Kami Huts [1]** follow the path that leads up a sandy scree slope on the west side of the valley to reach **Hausberg Col [2]**. Drop steeply down the other side on more sandy scree then boulders to reach **Oblong Tarn and Hausberg Tarn [3]**, (several excellent camping spots).

At this point this route divides; (ignore the path to the left which leads up to the left (east) of Arthur's Seat) take the path that leads straight on, between the tarns, to reach the foot of a scree slope and climbs steeply up scree to reach the **col [4]** on the ridge that extends westwards from Batian with Arthur's Seat and the Eastern Terminal, with Nanyuki Tarn at its base, are visible to the left (south).

The path trends left and downwards from the col passing below and to the cliffs below Arthur's Seat, then climbs up wide rock ledges towards the Eastern Terminal. To the right the entire length of the upper Hausberg Valley can be seen. To the left are steep rock walls. The path descends across bouldery scree to reach a rock platform then climbs, trending left, to reach **Nanyuki Tarn [5]**.

Pass to the left (north-east) of the tarn, to climb a short rocky section, then cross a small col to reach Hut Tarn. Pass to the right (west) of the tarn to reach **Two Tarn Hut [6]** (4990m).

Two Tarn Hut is built of corrugated iron, with a curved roof painted red, and can sleep 6 - 8 people. The door is not locked but the hut belongs to the Mountain Club of Kenya and walkers using it should obtain booking vouchers (40/-) from Naro Moru River Lodge or Let's Go Travel, Nairobi. Water is available from the tarn.

The hut is fairly clean and in good condition, probably because it is away from the main tourist routes; please help to keep it that way.

Two Tarn Hut to Austrian Hut
1¹/2 - 3 hours

From the **hut [1]** the path continues along the right (south) side of the tarn then drops steeply down a steep scree slope to **American Camp [2]**, a flat grassy area at the foot of a terminal moraine dropping down from the foot of the Tyndal Glacier. From American Camp a path trends right (south-west) to Teleki Lodge, Mackinder's Camp, and the start of the Naro Moru Route. Another path continues south-east (with the main summits up and to the left) to cross the head of the Teleki Valley and meet with the path coming up from Teleki Lodge and Mackinder's Camp leading towards Austrian Hut. The path can be seen zig-zagging up the large scree slope on the opposite side of the valley. Follow this clear path to reach **Austrian Hut [3]** (4790m). For details see the Naro Moru Route description.

Summit Circuit Route - Clockwise

Austrian Hut to Two Tarn Hut
1 - 1¹/2 hours

Leave **Austrian Hut [1]** in a southerly direction (i.e. with Point Lenana directly behind and the main summits up to the right) to cross a small plateau of boulders before trending down and rightwards towards the head of the Teleki Valley. The green roof of Teleki Lodge at Mackinder's Camp can be seen on the valley floor. The path is clear as it drops down scree, with the whole expanse of the Lewis Glacier visible to the right, to reach level vegetated ground at the head of the valley. To the right is a cliff split by a large fault with a cave at its base. The path divides; the path to the left leads down to Teleki Lodge and the Naro Moru Route, but keep trending right to cross a boggy area with small streams and climb a low ridge to reach **American Camp [2]**, a flat grassy area at the foot of a large bouldery terminal moraine extending down from the foot of the Tyndal Glacier.
From American Camp, the path climbs steeply up the right side of a scree slope aiming for the lowest point on the ridge that extends south-westerly from the main peaks. At the top of this ridge is Hut Tarn and **Two Tarn Hut [3]** (4490m). For details of the hut see the Summit Circuit (Anti-clockwise) Route description.

Two Tarn Hut to Kami Huts
2 - 3 hours

[1]

1.00

[2]

0.35

[3]

0.15

From **Two Tarn Hut [1]** aim northwards, along the left (west) side of the tarn. Directly ahead a ridge extends westward out from the shoulder of Point Pigott. At its western end this ridge drops sharply to form rocky cliffs. This is the Eastern Terminal and, further to the north, the Western Terminal. At the centre of the ridge, between two cols, is a minor peak called Arthur's Seat (see photo).

The path divides: the right fork leads across boulders up to a col between Arthur's Seat and the western shoulder of Point Pigott; the left fork leads to the other col, to the left (west) of Arthur's Seat and not clearly visible from this point. Follow the path on the left down to Nanyuki Tarn then below and to the left of the cliffs of the Eastern Terminal. Drop slightly, across wide rock ledges, then trend up and left round the base of the cliffs of Arthur's Seat to reach the col between Arthur's Seat and the Western Terminal.

From the col, Hausberg Tarn and Oblong Tarn are visible at the head of the Hausberg Valley. Drop down the scree and across easy ground to pass between the **tarns [2]**.

The path climbs over boulders then zig-zags up sandy scree to reach the **Hausberg Col [3]**, a low point in the ridge that extends northwards from the main peaks. From this point, the head of the Mackinder Valley (with the Sirimon Route) and the green roof of Shipton's Camp can be seen. Directly below the col, on the west side of the valley above Shipton's Camp, the conical tin roof of one of the Kami Huts is just visible.

Western Terminal and Arthur's Seat: From Two Tarn Hut

[4]
0.05
[5]

Drop down on sandy scree to reach **Kami Tarn [4]**, passed to the left, and Kami Huts (4590m). For details of **Kami Huts [5]** see the Sirimon Route description.

Kami Huts to Austrian Hut
2 - 3 hours

Visible from Kami Huts, at the head of the Mackinder Valley, a ridge extends north-east from Point Lenana. The main summits of Batian and Nelion are above and to the right.

[1]
1.00
[2]

From **Kami Huts [1]** the path aims east of south to contour along the side of the Mackinder valley, across a bouldery area then bare scree, below and to the left of steep brown cliffs, to meet the path coming steeply up the scree from Shipton's Camp. Follow this path (cairned) up the scree trending left where the path divides to reach the lowest point on the ridge. this is **Simba Col [2]**. Pass through the col and drop down to reach (Upper) Simba Tarn.

The path leading to Simba Col may be indistinct. If this path is missed, keep aiming straight up the path (cairned) to reach a point on the ridge to the right (south-east) of and higher than Simba Col. Just over the ridge is Harris Tarn, from where it is possible to turn left and drop down the scree to (Upper) Simba Tarn. Austrian Hut can be reached from either Simba Tarn or Harris Tarn (via Square Tarn and Tooth Col or via point Lenana). For details of these paths see the Sirimon Route section.

Descent routes from Austrian Hut

The Naro Moru Route
To reach the top of the Naro Moru Route, walkers should leave Austrian Hut following the directions in the Summit Circuit (Clockwise) Route description to reach the head of the Teleki Valley and Teleki Lodge/Mackinder's Camp (45 mins - 1 hour).

From Mackinder's Camp follow the clear path alongside the stream flowing down the centre of the valley floor. The path divides: left to cross the stream and climbs gently up the left (south) side of the valley; right to continue on the valley floor, crossing the stream and climbing steeply up the left side of the valley about 3km further down. The paths rejoin before dropping steeply through the area of tussock grass (swampy after rain) called the vertical bog. Red and white marker poles indicate the way. The path enters the forest and meets a rough drivable track which leads past the radio station to Met Station Camp ($3^1/2$ to 4 hours).

From the Met Station to Naro Moru Park Gate is 7km, and then a further 18km to Naro Moru town on a good drivable dirt road.

The Chogoria Route

To reach the top of the Chogoria Route walkers should leave Austrian Hut following the directions in the Summit Circuit (Anti-clockwise) Route description to reach Square Tarn (25 minutes).

At Simba Tarn the path divides: left to continue on the Summit Circuit Route; right to drop steeply down scree to the flat green area at the head of the Gorges Valley (Temple Fields). Hall Tarns and the sheer cliffs of The Temple can be clearly seen further down the valley. From Temple Fields keep to the clear path on the left (north) side of the valley to reach Hall Tarns and Minto's Hut (1 - 1^1/$_2$ hours). From Minto's to the roadhead is 2 - 3 hours' walking. From the roadhead to the park gate is 7km, and then a further 25km to Chogoria town.

The Sirimon Route

To reach the top of the Sirimon Route from Austrian Hut, walkers can follow the Summit Circuit Route in either direction to reach Shipton's Camp at the head of the Mackinder Valley (via Two Tarn Hut and Kami Huts 2 - 3 hours anti-clockwise, via Tooth Col and Simba Col 3 - 4^1/$_2$ hours clockwise). From Shipton's Camp follow the clear path down the valley, cross a stream and keep to the right (east) side of the valley to reach a fork (1^1/$_2$ – 2 hours). Both paths lead to Old Moses Camp.

a) The path to Liki North Hut contours along the valley side, passing a single red and white marker pole, then climbs steeply to the top of a ridge before dropping down, trending left then right into the valley. From Liki North Hut follow the path down the valley, cross the Liki North River, then trend up and right to a small col, before dropping down round the head of the next valley to follow a broad ridge down to meet a rough track which leads to Old Moses Camp and Judmeier Camp (4 – 5 hours).

b) The direct path drops towards the river then climbs following several red and white marker poles, to cross over a ridge and drops to cross the Liki North River before climbing again to reach a flatter area. The path meets a disused track. Turn right and follow this track, crossing the Ontulili River. Turn left onto the track and drop down to Old Moses Camp and Judmeier Camp (3 – 4 hours).

The Survival Club

for Adventure and Conservation

Morland, Cumbria CA10 3AZ
Tel 09314 483

Winter Mountaineering Skills
Rock Climbing Courses
Canoeing Courses
Paragliding Weekends
Snowdon Horseshoe

Ben Nevis Weekend
K2 Base Camp
Yosemite, USA
Island Peak, Nepal
magazine, gear discounts

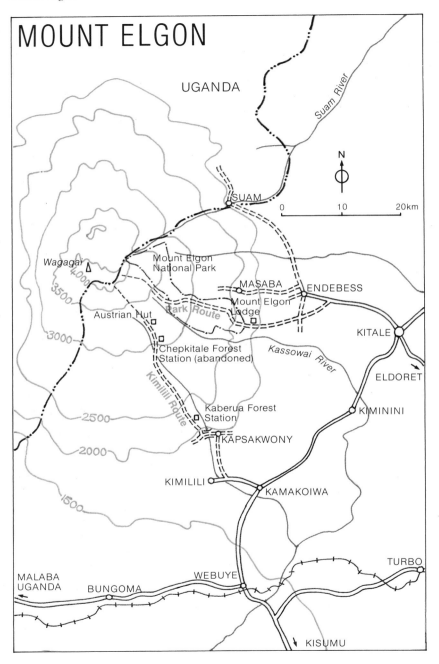

MOUNT ELGON

UGANDA

Suam River

N

0   10   20km

SUAM

Wagagai
4000
3500
Mount Elgon
National Park
MASABA   ENDEBESS
3000
Austrian Hut
Park Route
Mount Elgon
Lodge
KITALE
Chepkitale Forest
Station (abandoned)
Kassowai River
ELDORET
2500
Kimilili Route
Kaberua Forest
Station
KIMININI
KAPSAKWONY
2000
KIMILILI
KAMAKOIWA
1500
TURBO
MALABA
UGANDA
WEBUYE
BUNGOMA
KISUMU

Mount Elgon

Mount Elgon is the second highest mountain in Kenya and, like many other East African peaks, is the remains of an ancient volcano, but at just over 4300m/14,000ft this mountain has been spared the severe erosion by snow and ice which formed the more pointed peaks of Mount Kenya. At its base, though, Mount Elgon is even wider than Mount Kenya which indicates to geologists that at one time Mount Elgon may have been the highest mountain in Africa.

The famous explorer, Henry Stanley, is thought to have seen Mount Kenya from a distance while travelling in the regions around Lake Victoria in 1878. A later explorer, Joseph Thomson, reached this region in 1883 and climbed through the forest to the caves on the southern side of the mountain. Before the Europeans arrived, the mountain was inhabited by a group of people called the El Kony, whose name drives from the Maasai word for the mountain, Ol Doinyo Ilgoon, meaning mountain shaped like a breast. Until the early 1960s some El Kony people were still living in caves on the mountain.

At the centre of Mount Elgon's peak area is a large distinct crater (more correctly called a caldera). Walkers can reach the rim and descend down onto the crater floor itself. This is perfectly safe as the volcano is now extinct; the only volcanic activity evident today are some hot springs that emerge from the crater floor, forming an additional attraction and a good place for a dip after a warm morning's walking.

Mount Elgon is in the far west of the country, and the border between Kenya and Uganda passes through the crater. At least one route up to the crater exists on the Ugandan side of the mountain, but only the routes on the Kenyan side are covered in this book. In recent years Uganda has suffered considerably from the effects of civil war and other internal political troubles, and the country has been officially closed to tourists. Even when the border is open very few visitors travel through Uganda, and even less climb on the Ugandan side of Mount Elgon.

The crater rim of Mount Elgon is surmounted by a ring of large, 'tabular' (flat-topped, steep-sided), peaks. The highest of these peaks, Wagagai (4321m), is in Ugandan territory, while the second highest, Lower Elgon (4301m), is split by the Kenya-Uganda border. The highest peak totally within Kenya is Koitoboss (4187m) on the western side of the mountain.

The area around Mount Elgon is mainly farmland. Plantations and shambas have been established on the lower slopes, while large areas of land designated as forest reserve cover the hills higher up. The surrounding region has a fairly dense rural population and communications between Nairobi and the main towns of the region, Kitale and Webuye, are good.

Note that in some guidebooks Lower Elgon Peak is referred to as Sudek, although on most maps Sudek is indicated as a distinct lower peak lying just to the south of Lower Elgon Peak and separated from it by a col or large gap.

Best time to visit

During the rainy seasons the approach routes, on dirt roads through farmland and forest, are usually impassable. The rainiest months are usually April to May and August to November. Water supplies on the higher parts of Mount Elgon are not reliable throughout the year so the best time to visit is just after the rainy season when the approach routes have dried out but the streams and springs are still full of water.

Nights in the crater (just under 4000m) are often below freezing and sharp frosts are common. Even during the 'warm' or 'dry' seasons snow or hail often falls in the crater or around the main peaks.

As on any mountain, however, the seasons and weather conditions are never completely predictable. At any time of the year walkers should be prepared for periods of unusually wet, or dry, weather and take adequate protective clothing.

Special conditions

A section of Mount Elgon's slopes, on the north-eastern part of the Kenyan side, has been gazetted as a national park. The crater and peak area of Mount Elgon are outside the national park boundary, but one route up to the crater passes through the park which visitors are not allowed to enter without a vehicle. The main entrance gate to the park is guarded by rangers and all fees are payable here. The park has two other gates; these are unguarded and closed to the public.

The Mount Elgon Reserve and National Park were gazetted to protect the forest and moorland inhabited by numerous species of animal including elephant, buffalo, forest hog, waterbuck, bushbuck, duiker and colobus monkey. The elephants this area are particularly remarkable; using their tusks to break off large pieces of rock from large caves in the mountainside which they then lick or eat to obtain vital mineral salts. So much rock has been removed by the elephants that the largest caves are now many hundreds of metres deep. Unfortunately, the Mount Elgon elephant population has been heavily poached in recent years and the remaining elephants are now very wary of humans and unlikely to be seen.

Visitors driving through the park can leave their vehicle to visit the caves. The largest cave, Makingeny, and the second largest, Kitum, are both clearly signposted, a short walk up a footpath from the park track.

Walkers without their own vehicle can still reach the crater area by following the Kimilili Route which approaches the crater area from the southern side of the mountain, outside the national park boundary.

Warnings

During the Ugandan civil war, rebel soldiers crossed Mount Elgon into Kenyan territory and a number of atrocities were committed. The poachers hunting for elephants in this region were also particularly ruthless, and during the mid-1980s walkers were not allowed to visit the crater and main peak area. Since the war has ended in Uganda and the elephants have been virtually exterminated, visitors are unlikely to encounter rebels or poachers. However, a case was reported in late 1989 where a Kenyan army patrol shot at two walkers on the Kimilili Route mistaking them for Ugandan insurgents. This was obviously an isolated incident, and the walkers involved were not harmed, but visitors should be aware that they walk on Mount Elgon at their own risk, however slight, and with a certain degree of discretion. Tourists passing through the national park on their way to the start of the Park Route up to the crater are officially required to take a park ranger to act as guard and/or guide, but this is not the case for walkers using the Kimilili Route.

General approaches
The Mount Elgon massif lies about 350km to the north-west of Nairobi. The easiest route for driving is via the large towns of Nakuru and Eldoret. About 15km beyond Eldoret the main road forks. To reach the southern side of the mountain (for the Kimilili Route) keep left on the Malaba/Uganda border road to Webuye. In Webuye turn right on to the Kitale road and after 20km turn left for Kimilili. To reach the eastern side of the mountain (for the Park Route) turn right at the fork to Kitale. In Kitale go straight on through the town on the Suam/Uganda border road to Enderbess. These routes are all tarred and generally in good condition. Petrol is available in the main towns.

Buses run regularly (at least two each day) from Nairobi to Eldoret, Webuye and Kitale. Hitching is also possible along these main roads. Matatus run from Webuye to Kimilili and from Kitale to Enderbess.

The routes
Two routes up to the crater rim are described. The mountain can be traversed by combining these two routes, and another that crosses the crater, so each route is described in both directions.

A point of interest is the hot springs inside the crater, which are best approached from Koitoboss Col, at the top of the Park Route. This route is also described.

Walkers traversing the mountain should remember that on the Park Route walking is not permitted within the national park itself. Walkers should arrange for a vehicle to pick them up or drop them off on the park side. Alternatively, it is possible to descend the Park Route and leave the park by one of the unguarded gates, although this is illegal. Walkers may encounter forest rangers who patrol the forest reserve outside the national park and a certain degree of diplomacy may be required to avoid problems.

Maps
The peak area and western approaches to Mount Elgon are covered by the SK Series Y503 1:250M sheet NA-36-12 (Kapenguria), which also shows

the Cheranganis. For more detail, the crater and tops of the Park and Kimilili Routes are also covered by SK Series Y731 1:50M sheet 74/3 (Elgony). This map may be difficult to obtain, however, as it shows a border area and is considered a security risk. The *Mount Elgon Map and Guide*, published by A. Wielochowski, is available in Nairobi and Britain (see the Maps section on p55 for more details).

The Kimilili Route

The Kimilili Route starts at Kaberua Forest Station (formerly Kimilili Forest Station) on the southern side of Mount Elgon, about 12km from the small town of Kimilili, and about 35km north of Webuye.

This route leads to the crater rim near Lower Elgon Peak, and is more suitable than the Park Route for walkers without their own transport as it does not pass through national park land and a vehicle is not officially required. For drivers the 29km of dirt track from Kaberua Forest Station to the roadhead at 3350m takes 3 - 4 hours. Walkers without a vehicle should allow 8 - 11 hours. This can be split over two days as there are a number of suitable camping places en route.

At the 3350m roadhead there is a ruined hut and a camping place. From the roadhead to Lower Elgon Peak is 4 - 5 hours' walking.

Approach and formalities

To reach Kaberua Forest Station drivers should turn off (west) the main Kitale - Webuye road at Kamakoiwa, signposted towards Kimilili. After 6.5km turn right (north) onto a dirt road, signposted Kapsakwony High School, and follow this road for 9km to reach Kapsakwony. Drive up the main street, left at a T-junction, then follow this dirt road, over a bridge, to turn right (north) after 2.5km. Kaberua Forest Station is signposted and reached after a further 2.5km.

Local matatus run between Kamakoiwa, Kimilili and Kapsakwony, and occasionally on to Kaberua.

Kimilili town has a market, shops and basic lodging houses. A wider selection of goods and places to sleep is available in Kitale or Webuye.

At Kaberua Forest Station visitors should report to the Rangers Office, beyond the village on the right side of the track just before a wooden barrier pole, to pay an entrance fee (5/- ppn). If you are going up and coming down the same way, surplus gear can be stored here.

Kaberua - The roadhead and hut

From Kaberua Forest Station the drivable track continues northwards through plantation, forest and bamboo and finally out onto open heathland. The track is generally easy to follow, and although eroded in places, it is generally passable for 4WD vehicles. Since Chepkitale Forest Station was abandoned this track receives little traffic and may become increasingly overgrown. Two minor tracks join the main track but should

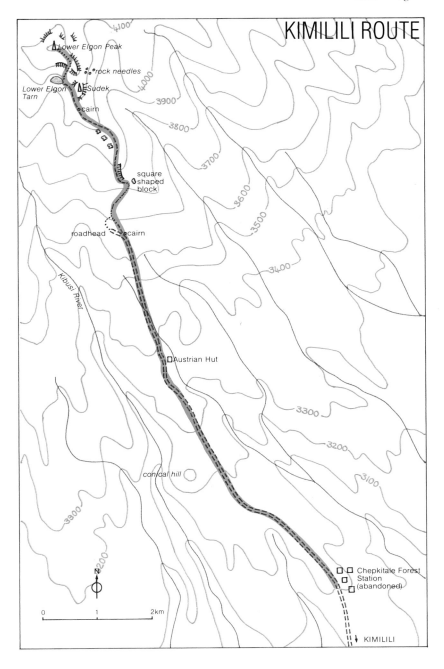

KIMILILI ROUTE

Lower Elgon Peak

rock needles

Sudek

Lower Elgon Tarn

cairn

square shaped block

roadhead   cairn

Kibusi River

Austrian Hut

conical hill

Chepkitale Forest Station (abandoned)

N

0   1   2km

↓ KIMILILI

not cause any confusion; keep heading uphill. For walkers breaking the journey there are many suitable camping places. It is also possible to sleep in the abandoned buildings at Chepkitale Forest Station (reached after 22km); there is plenty of firewood here (the wooden huts are slowly being dismantled) but the water supply is unreliable. Water is available on the way up from two streams (11km and 19km from Kaberua) crossed by earth embankments.

At Chepkitale walkers get their first view of the main peaks as the track continues through more open country. If the track becomes indistinct it is important to keep to the ridges and not drop down into the wooded valleys on either side. The track divides near a prominent conical hill where the left fork drops down into the valley towards the base of the hill; take the right fork and keep gaining height.

The roadhead and hut at 3350m are 7km from Chepkitale; 2 - 3 hours' walking and $1^{1}/_{2}$ hours' drive. Although the hut itself is now lacking a roof, and most of the furniture has been burnt, the fireplace is still intact and the surrounding flat grassy area is good for camping. Water is available from a stream 5 minutes' walk down into the valley behind the hut.

Before falling again into disrepair the hut was rebuilt in 1985 by British and Austrian volunteers working in the area. It therefore became known as Austrian Hut and is marked as such on some recent maps and guidebooks.

Austrian Hut to Lower Elgon Tarn
$2^{1}/_{2}$ - $3^{1}/_{2}$ hours 700m

To help orientation the view from the hut is described. The highest peak visible on the skyline (i.e. the one that appears highest) is a large flat-topped rocky buttress composed of fluted vertical columns with a conical point on its leftward end; this is Lower Elgon Peak. In front of this is the smaller square-shaped buttress of Sudek. To the right a pointed mushroom-shaped rock tower is visible in the gap in the skyline. The path follows a broad ridge and aims first towards this gap then, nearer the top, trends left to aim for the left side of Sudek. The path then goes over the left shoulder of Sudek and to the left of the main buttress of Lower Elgon (see photo opposite).

From the **hut [1]** the track continues through grassy moorland. It is possible to drive 3.2km further to a point (marked by a **cairn and pole [2]**) where the path leaves the track on its right side. The drivable track continues for another 0.5km to a vague roadhead from where an indistinct path meets the path coming up from the cairn. Both paths and the track are indistinct for a short section as they cross rocky ground. The path continues up the broad ridge, marked in places by small cairns and occasional splashes of white paint, trending to the left side of the ridge, then to the right to keep above a

Lower Elgon Peak, viewed from Austrian Hut

steep, thickly vegetated valley to the left. Again the path is indistinct; aim towards a **square-shaped block [3]** (about 10m high) visible about 300m away in a low gap in the skyline. From this block trend left then right round the base of a hill to follow the path below and to left of **cliffs [4]**, from the end of which Lower Elgon Peak and Sudek can be clearly seen. Contrary to expectation, the path does not aim directly towards Sudek but trends right, to the other side of the broad ridge to pass to the right of a group of rocky outcrops (running in a line along the crest of the ridge). To the right (east) is a large steep-sided valley. Ahead, a group of large rock needles and spires can be seen to the right of the main buttress of Lower Elgon Peak.

The path climbs fairly steeply up the right side of the broad ridge then trends back to the left side to climb up to a cairn and pole on the left **shoulder of Sudek [5]**. From this point the wide gap between Lower Elgon and Sudek can be seen. Descend steeply from the shoulder then follow the path as it trends left, keeping below and to the left of Sudek and Lower Elgon. A few cairns mark the path as it crosses some patches of exposed rock to reach **Lower Elgon Tarn [6]**, hidden in a shallow corrie (4140m).

Lower Elgon Tarn to Lower Elgon Peak
30 mins 160m

From the **tarn [1]** a steep vegetated gulley can be seen, to the left of the highest cliffs, leading to a low point in the plateau on top of Lower Elgon Peak. Scramble up this with care to the low point then turn left (north-west) to follow small cairns to

[2]
0.05
[3]

the **summit [2]** (4301m/14,111ft), marked by a large cairn and pole. From the summit continue in the same direction to a spectacular **viewpoint [3]** overlooking the main caldera.

For a day-hike from Austrian Hut the tarn makes a fine picnic spot and, before descending, the extra distance up to the summit of Lower Elgon Peak makes the walk especially rewarding.

From this point it is also possible to traverse the mountain to Koitoboss Col and descend by the Park Route and these routes are described in later sections of this chapter.

Lower Elgon Peak and Tarn to Austrian Hut
2¹/2 - 3¹/2 hours Descent Route

[1]
0.30
[2]
0.30
[3]
[4]
0.15
[5]
0.10
[6]
0.20
[7]
0.10
[8]
0.45

From the **summit [1]** of Lower Elgon small cairns mark the path aiming south-east to a low point in the plateau. To the right (south-west) a steep vegetated gulley leads down to **Lower Elgon Tarn [2]**.

From the tarn follow small cairns south-easterly across rocky ground. A wide gap separates Lower Elgon from another large buttress; Sudek. Keeping Lower Elgon and Sudek to the left the path climbs steeply to the right **shoulder of Sudek [3]**, marked by a large cairn and pole.

To help orientation, from this point it is possible to see a flat-topped conical hill about 9km distant, slightly east of south, at the end of a broad ridge. (There are a number of conical hills visible, but this is the only one with very few trees on top.) The hut is reached before this hill, but it provides a useful reference point. It is important to keep to the broad ridge and not descend into the valleys on either side.

Follow the path from the **shoulder of Sudek [4]** down the ridge, keeping left of a line of rocky outcrops that run down the crest of the main ridge. To the left is a large steep-sided valley. Directly behind, on the right (east) side of Lower Elgon, a group of large impressive rock towers and needles is visible.

The **path trends over to the right side of the ridge [5]**, passing to the right of cliffs. Beyond the cliffs the path becomes indistinct. Trend left, to avoid dropping into a small vegetated valley, and aim towards a **square-shaped block [6]** (about 10m high) in a gap about 300m away, then trend right and down slightly to pick up the path and continue down the right side of the broad ridge.

Cross a **rocky section [7]**, where the path becomes indistinct, and continue down the ridge to rejoin either the faint drivable track or the path which meet by a **cairn [8]**. Follow the

[9]

drivable track down through grassy moorland. Two paths cross the track almost perpendicularly but keep to the track to reach the **Austrian Hut [9]**, (for full details see the ascent route description).

Austrian Hut to Kaberua Forest Station
Descent route

The drivable track is used very infrequently by vehicles and is badly eroded and overgrown in places, but is generally easy to follow. The abandoned Chepkitale Forest Station is reached after 7km ($1^1/_2$ - 2 hours). The track forks 10km below Chepkitale; take the lower fork to the left. Half a kilometre farther at a second fork keep right to stay on the main track. Descend through bamboo, forest, then plantation to reach Kaberua.

The total distance is 29km; 4 - 5 hours driving, 7 - 9 hours walking. Walkers can split this over two days, by stopping at Chepkitale or a number of suitable camping places en route. The track crosses streams 3km and 11km below Chepkitale, (for full details see the ascent route description).

Across the crater

Any paths that do exist in the crater of Mount Elgon are invariably indistinct and difficult to follow. Walkers frequently have to make their own way through giant groundsel 'forest' and across thick beds of tussock

Lower Elgon Tarn

Groundsels in Elgon Crater

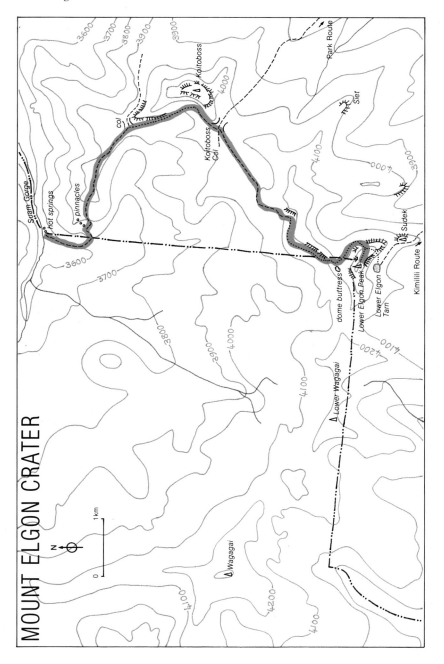

MOUNT ELGON CRATER

grass and heather. It is often necessary to rely on various landmarks around the crater for orientation and to confirm position. Inexperienced mountain walkers are advised not to attempt these routes if the weather is bad and visibility poor.

Lower Elgon Peak to Koitoboss Col
2 - 3 hours

From the viewpoint at the north-western end of Lower Elgon Peak it is possible to see a large dome buttress separated from the main buttress of Lower Elgon by a col.

[1]

0.40

[2]

1.00

[3]

0.10

[4]

0.35

[5]

From the **summit [1]**, retrace to the low point in the plateau and turn left (north-east) to descend by a series of ramps and gulleys into the valley, then trend left to climb the head of the valley to reach the **crater rim[2]** on the right (north-east) side of the dome buttress. There is no path and care should be taken on the descent.

From the dome buttress keep the inside of the crater to the left and the head of the steep valley to the right. At a rocky buttress in the crest of the rim, trend left and down towards the crater floor on a poorly defined path. Do not follow this path down but trend right, away from it, to maintain the contour. There is no path and it is necessary to wade through heather between the giant groundsels but, because the way is generally level, the going is not too strenuous. Continue trending right, maintaining height, and passing below and to the left of grey rocky buttresses on the skyline, to reach the head of a small valley. Cross a small stream then trend left, passing below and to left of a series of **low vegetated cliffs [3]** (some overhanging).

The path climbs out of this valley, trending up and right, to reach the **crest of a spur [4]** sloping down right to left towards the centre of the crater. Cross this spur and, keeping level, pass the head of a large steep-sided valley to the left.

Another spur (short and rocky, and also sloping down right to left) is reached. From here it is possible to see across a flat area of tussock grass, beyond which is a mound edged with low cliffs, and beyond that the large fluted block of Koitoboss Peak is clearly visible.

The path crosses the tussock grass and climbs the right end of the mound. Passing well to the left of the inner wall of the crater, cross boggy sections of tussock grass and rocky 'islands' above the swampy areas. Follow the path north-east, aiming directly for Koitoboss Peak. **Koitoboss Col [5]** is at the south-western end of Koitoboss Peak.

Koitoboss Col to Lower Elgon Peak and Lower Elgon Tarn
2^1/2 - 4 hours

Lower Elgon Peak cannot be seen from Koitoboss Col, but it lies to the left (east) of Lower Wagagai Peak which can be seen to the south-west of Koitoboss on the other side of the crater.

[1]
0.25
[2]
0.15
[3]
0.10
[4]
0.05
[5]
0.40
[6]
0.30
[7]
1.00
[8]

From the southern side of **Koitoboss Col [1]** (facing into the crater), a path can be seen running south-easterly across the crater floor inside and to the right of the hills that form the crater rim. This path reaches a low elongated rock platform and follows the top of this to keep above patches of swampy tussock grass. This platform joins a larger groundsel-covered mound, and the path drops down off this mound and crosses an area of boggy ground.

A **ridge [2]** is reached, sloping down left to right in towards the crater centre. Cross this ridge and continue to contour passing to the left of the **head of a broad steep-sided valley [3]**. There is no path but trend left and down through heather into the head of a small valley to pass below and to the right of a series of **low vegetated cliffs [4]** (some overhanging). Continue to trend right, round the head of the valley, cross a **small stream [5]**, and contour round the inside of the crater wall passing below and to the right of high rocky buttresses on the skyline and an area of scattered boulders below them. Keep level or gain height gradually to reach the crest of a **small spur [6]** from where Lower Elgon Peak is visible.

To the right (north) end of Lower Elgon is a large dome buttress. Aim towards this to cut across a path leading up to the ridge from the crater floor. Follow this path to a low point on the **crater rim [7]** to the left (north) of the dome buttress. Keep to the rim, then trend left round the head of a steep-sided valley, with a stream at its bottom (flowing south-easterly), to a point below a series of ramps and gulleys. Scramble up to the plateau on top of Lower Elgon Peak. A large cairn marks the actual **summit [8]**.

Lower Elgon Tarn can be reached from the summit (see the Kimilili Route description for full details).

[9]
0.20
[10]
0.15
[11]

It is also possible to reach the tarn by passing below and to the right of the **dome buttress [9]**, then aiming for the lowest point of the wide col between Lower Elgon and Wagagai Peaks. Pass through the **col [10]** onto the outer wall of the crater then trend left and downwards across flat terraces to reach **Lower Elgon Tarn [11]**.

Do not attempt to pass through the narrow cleft separating the main part of Lower Elgon Peak from its subsidiary buttress on the right. This will bring you out too high above the tarn and the way down is very steep.

The Park Route

The Park Route starts at the small centre of Endebess, on the eastern side of Mount Elgon, about 15km north-west of Kitale, and joins the crater rim at Koitoboss Col.

The 25km of dirt track from Endebess to the roadhead (steep in places - 4WD an advantage) takes about four hours driving, and from the roadhead at 3500m to the crater rim is a 3 - 4 hour walk. There are no huts on this route, although there are some good campsites in the park and another good camping place at the roadhead.

As the route passes through the Mount Elgon National Park a vehicle is essential to reach the roadhead and the beginning of the trail up to the crater. (The drivable track crosses the boundary before the roadhead so the walking section is outside the park.)

Approach and formalities

The entrance to the Mount Elgon National Park is Chorlim Gate, about 12km from Endebess. The tarred road from Kitale ends at Endebess (20km). Near the post office two dirt tracks lead up towards the mountain. Take the one on the left. After 5km turn right at a crossroads and follow this track for 7km through shambas and farmland to the park gate. About 1km before the gate the Mount Elgon Lodge is passed on the right.

It is also possible to reach Chorlim Gate by turning left off the Kitale - Endebess road about 10km outside Kitale. Follow this track for about 9km, straight on at the crossroads, then for 7km, as above, to the park gate. The park is signposted on both of these approach routes.

There is no public transport to the park gate. Matatus run from Kitale to Endebess, from where it is possible to walk through the farmland to the park gate. Mount Elgon National Park receives few visitors so the chance of hitching a ride into the park is slight. A lift to the roadhead would be even more unlikely.

There is no ideal base at the start of this route but basic lodgings and supplies can be found in Kitale. Accommodation is also available at the Mount Elgon Lodge, near the park gate, once a spacious settler farmhouse and now a quiet hotel with pleasant gardens and excellent views over the surrounding countryside (d 910/- fb, 1990). Enquiries to Mount Elgon Lodge, PO Box 7, Endebess, Kitale, or Msafiri Inns, PO Box 42013, Utalii House, Uhuru Highway, Nairobi, Tel 29751, 330820, 23488.

Camping is permitted on a patch of grass outside the park gate. Water is available and there is a small shop in the rangers, compound nearby.

Chorlim Gate is permanently guarded by park rangers and entrance is

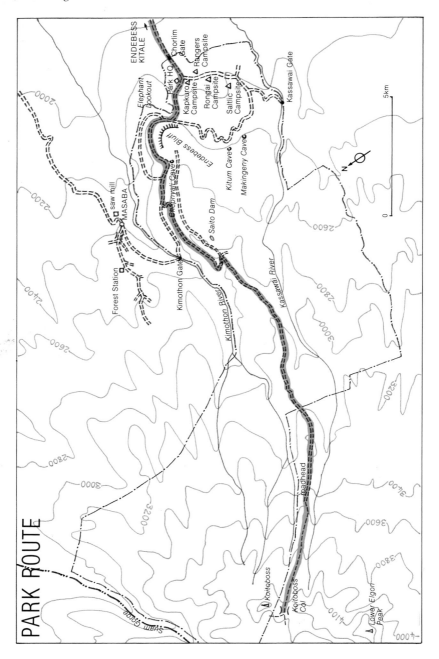

PARK ROUTE

permitted between 6 a.m. and 6 p.m. only. The two other entrances into the park at Kimothon Gate and Kassawai Gate are not guarded but access is permitted for official vehicles only. With permission from the rangers at Chorlim Gate tourist vehicles may be allowed to leave the park via one of these other gates.

The rangers at Chorlim Gate emphasize that walking inside the park is not permitted, and also recommend that walkers on the path from the roadhead to the crater rim (even though this is outside the park boundary) are accompanied by a ranger to act as guide and/or guard. Generally, though, the rangers' knowledge of the routes beyond the roadhead (and the times and distances involved) is scanty and unreliable. Also, unless special arrangements are made to provide food and equipment for the ranger, it will be necessary to return to the gate within a day. Walkers who intend to walk beyond the roadhead, and who feel that an accompanying ranger is unnecessary, should do so with discretion.

Through the park

From the park gate various tracks run through the park, all leading eventually to one track which leads up the mountain to the roadhead. Koitoboss Peak is clearly signposted at all junctions but the distances shown are only to the roadhead, and even these are underestimated. From the gate to the roadhead by the shortest route is 33km. This is 2 - 4 hours' drive, depending on conditions. The track is steep and badly eroded in places so that after the rains it is often impassable.

The Roadhead to Koitoboss Col
2 – 3 hours 500m

[1]
0.15
[2]

0.45

[3]

0.30
[4]

From the **roadhead [1]** a path leads directly up towards the top of the ridge, crossing several steep patches of bare rock, but keeps below the top, passing below and to the right of the rock outcrop at the head of the ridge. To the right is the steep Kimothon Valley. The path continues up the right (east) side of the ridge, climbing gradually, passing below and to the right of a series of grey and orange **rock buttresses [2]** and balancing boulders. At around this point Koitoboss Peak can be seen; a long, flat-topped, rock buttress composed of vertical fluted columns, with a rounded peak at its left (southern) end. The path divides into game trails, and is boggy in places, but continues to climb the right side of the ridge to reach the broad crest near a **buttress [3]** with a square block on its left side and a number of smaller pinnacles on its right. Pass to the left of this buttress to continue up the left side of the ridge, then along the crest, to pass below and to the right of a group of **standing boulders [4]** at the head of a higher ridge. Follow

the path (which divides into game trails in places) along the right side of this higher ridge, still keeping the Kimothon Valley down to the right, aiming towards the left side of the col which is clearly visible to the left of Koitoboss Peak. To the left of the lowest point of the col is a small rocky mound. The path passes to the left of this mound and crosses the **crater rim [5]** (3990m).

From Koitoboss Col it is possible to see (from left to right, clockwise around the crater rim) the main peaks of Lower Wagagai and Wagagai with the lower peaks in between, the large gap between Jackson's Summit and Mubiyi Peak, and the head of the Suam Gorge.

For a day-hike from the roadhead this point makes a good half-way point. Alternatively, walkers can go farther to visit the hot springs (described later) or complete a traverse of the mountain and descend on the Kimilili Route (described previously). The route from Koitoboss Col down to the park roadhead is also described mainly for those doing a traverse of the mountain having come up the Kimilili Route, but it may also be useful for walkers who have already ascended by this route.

Koitoboss Col to The Hot Springs
2 - 3 hours

From **Koitoboss Col [1]**, pass inside the crater wall, below and to the left of the main cliffs of Koitoboss Peak. The path is indistinct in places but the way continues to curve, trending left, parallel to the curve of the inner wall of the crater. Keep to the heather, rather than the tussock grass on the lower, flatter, ground.

The way passes to the left of another **col [2]** in the crater wall, between the cliffs extending leftwards from the peak of Koitoboss and a smaller conical hill. Join the path which comes into the crater through this col, and keep to it as it contours round the left side of the conical hill and leads out along the crest of a **broad ridge [3]** projecting in towards the centre of the crater. The path climbs and drops as it surmounts small knolls on the ridge.

At the head of the ridge the path drops steeply. To the right is the head of the Suam Gorge, but the path trends to the left, then to the right passing to the left of a group of prominent **rock pinnacles [4]**, then trending right, below and to the left of the pinnacles, onto the crater floor.

A large stream flows across the crater floor into the Suam Gorge. Cross the stream to the base of the steep hillside on the opposite (north) bank. Below some patches of bare rock, streaked black and white, the hot water bubbles up into numerous **pools [5]** then flows out to mix with the cold

The Hot Springs   *Bamboo on The Aberdares*

[5]

stream water. The supply of hot water seems to vary so the pools are sometimes quite shallow and only good for dipping your feet in, although this is very refreshing after a long walk round the crater.

Return to Koitoboss Col by the same route ($2^1/2$ - $3^1/2$ hours).

Koitoboss Col to The Park Roadhead
1 - 2 hours Descent Route

[1]
0.15

[2]

0.20

[3]

0.40

[4]

The path down to the roadhead passes through **Koitoboss Col [1]** at its right side (looking out of the crater, to the south-east), and leads down the left side of a ridge, keeping a shallow valley to the left. The path divides into numerous game trails, and is boggy in places, but continues to drop gradually towards a group of **standing boulders [2]** visible at the head of the ridge.

At the boulders the path splits: the left fork passes below and to left of the boulders down the left side of the ridge; the right fork stays higher on the ridge and passes between the boulders. The paths rejoin and the main path continues along the crest of the broad ridge, then passes to the right of a **buttress [3]** topped by pinnacles and a square block.

After the buttress the path splits. Take the left fork down the left side of the ridge, passing below and to the left of a series of grey and orange buttresses and towers. The path divides into numerous boggy game trails but continues to drop gradually until a final steep descent, over patches of bare rock, to the **roadhead [4]**.

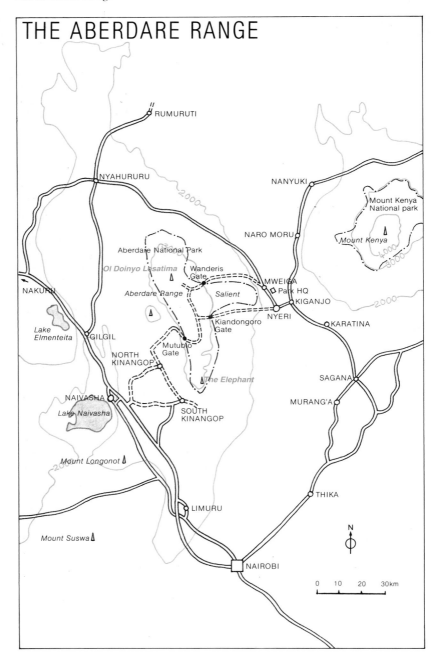

THE ABERDARE RANGE

RUMURUTI

NYAHURURU

NANYUKI

Mount Kenya
National park

NARO MORU

Mount Kenya

Aberdare National Park

Ol Doinyo Lesatima

Wanderis
Gate

MWEIGA

NAKURU

Aberdare Range

Salient

Park HQ

KIGANJO

NYERI

KARATINA

Kiandongoro
Gate

Lake
Elementeita

GILGIL

Mutubio
Gate

NORTH
KINANGOP

SAGANA

The Elephant

NAIVASHA

MURANG'A

Lake Naivasha

SOUTH
KINANGOP

Mount Longonot

THIKA

LIMURU

N

Mount Suswa

NAIROBI

0   10   20   30km

The Aberdare Range

The Aberdare Range (usually shortened to 'the Aberdares') is an elongated massif, running approximately north-south parallel to the direction of the Rift Valley, about 50km to the west of Mount Kenya. The steep western side of the range forms the eastern wall of this part of the Rift and the massifs of Mount Kenya and the Aberdares together form the Central Highlands.

Between the Aberdares and Mount Kenya is a broad plain intersected by numerous steep-sided valleys cut by the fast flowing rivers that run off the mountainsides. This region is the heartland of the Kikuyu people. The fertile soils and favourable conditions for farming support a growing population and it is one of the most densely populated rural regions in Kenya.

This region, at the foot of the Aberdares, had been cleared of forest and used for cultivation long before the explorer Joseph Thomson, the first European to see the range, reached this area in 1883. He named the range for Lord Aberdare, the president of the Royal Geographical Society. The local name for the range was Nyandarua, meaning 'drying hide'. (The Kikuyu people traditionally dried an animal hide by pegging out its edges and putting short poles under the spine to lift it off the ground. The shape of the range resembles a hide being dried in this way.)

In the 1930s an estate in the Wanjohi Valley, on the eastern side of the Aberdares, was the infamous retreat of a group of pleasure-seeking British aristocrats. One of the leading figures of this group was Josslyn Hay, Earl of Errol. His mysterious murder in 1941 added to the notoriety of 'Happy Valley', inspiring the book, and later the film, *White Mischief*.

During the colonial era, because the slopes of the Aberdares are steep and densely forested, the region was not settled and farmed by Europeans as extensively as on Mount Kenya. The scattered European population and the dense forest made the Aberdares an ideal base and hiding-ground for the anti-colonial Mau Mau guerillas who fought against the British in the 1950s during 'the Emergency'.

Since independence a section of the Aberdare Range has been gazetted as a national park. The park consists mainly of bamboo and high heath and moorland, but also contains large areas of forest, particularly in The Salient which extends eastwards from the main peaks and drops to a level of around 1500 metres. This area is inhabited by numerous species of animal, including 'the big five' (buffalo, rhino, elephant, leopard and lion), and also contains the famous 'tree hotels', Treetops and The Ark. Consequently, most visitors remain in the Salient area and do not venture onto the high moorland.

It is these high moorland zones, over 3000m, which offer the best conditions for walkers. The area is completely uninhabited, the walking is across fine open country, and the views (weather permitting) are superb.

The highest point of the Aberdares is Ol Doinyo Lesatima (often shortened to Satima) which, at 3999m/13,120ft, is the third highest peak in Kenya after Batian on Mount Kenya and Lower Wagagai on Mount Elgon. Like many East African mountains, the Aberdares were formed by volcanic activity but, whereas the conical shapes of Mount Kenya and Mount Elgon were created by eruptions from a central vent, the elongated form of the Aberdares is a result of lava spilling from large cracks or fissures. Consequently the main peaks of the Aberdare Range run in an almost straight line linked by a series of ridges which can be reached by walkers, but because the entire range lies within the national park, access is restricted to visitors with a vehicle and all walkers must be accompanied by a park ranger to act as guide and/or guard. It is possible, however, for the southern peaks of Kinangop and The Elephant to be approached without a vehicle.

Officially, the Aberdare Range has been renamed, and the original African name of Nyandarua reinstated, but the title of the national park remains unchanged and so the the range itself is still usually referred to as the Aberdares.

Best time to visit
The Aberdares are notoriously wet. Even in the dry seasons, while the rest of Kenya enjoys fine weather or only occasional downpours, the Aberdare Range is frequently enveloped in heavy rain cloud. During these periods of bad weather the dirt tracks are often impassable and the national park is closed. Mists are also frequent making route finding difficult. Weather conditions are less likely to be unfavourable from late December to mid-February, and during August and September.

Special conditions
Gates are positioned where the drivable tracks enter the national park land and all fees are payable here.

Unaccompanied walking is not officially allowed inside the park but, with permission, and escorted by an experienced park ranger, walkers can leave their vehicles and cross the moorland to any of the peaks. To arrange an escort write to The Warden, Aberdare National Park, PO Box 22, Nyeri, stating the dates of the visit, the number of people in the group and the intended destination. Include a reply address and allow at least two weeks for the request to be processed.

The authorities refer to any organized walking in the national park as 'trekking'. Two of the most popular routes are to the summit of Satima from the Wanderis track roadhead, and to the summit of Kinangop from the Fishing Lodge Bandas. Visitors normally arrange to collect their accompanying ranger from the national park HQ in Mweiga (10km north of Nyeri), and carry him in their vehicle to the start of the walk. The charge for this service is 30/- per day for each person in the group. For treks of longer than one day the ranger must be provided with food and tent. Tips are at the visitors' discretion. Requirements for each trek are likely to be different and should be arranged with the park HQ.

In the past walkers have reached the summit of Satima from the Wanderis track roadhead without a ranger escort, although this is illegal.

Warnings

Wild animals are mainly concentrated in the Salient area, especially around The Ark and Treetops lodges, where they are attracted by waterholes and saltlicks. However, some animals do reach the high moorland areas. In 1984 a woman tourist was savaged by a lion at Chania Falls campsite which resulted in the closure of all the campsites on the high moorland areas of the Aberdare National Park. Reports indicate that the lion had been released from a film set, and was confused by its surroundings, or that the woman may even have approached the lion. While such an encounter on the high moorland is extremely unlikely walkers should be prepared for surprise meetings with other large animals, particularly buffalo.

General approaches

The Aberdare massif extends over a wide area, but the highlands and peaks of the range itself lie about 80km to the north of Nairobi. It is possible to approach from many directions, but the best approach for Satima and the northern peaks is from Nyeri which is most easily reached from Nairobi via Thika and Karatina. Avoid the road through Murang'a, as it is in bad condition (March 1990). The roads are tarred and petrol is available.

From Nyeri numerous drivable tracks enter the national park and lead to the Salient or up to the high moorlands. At any time of year four-wheel drive vehicles, although not essential, are highly recommended.

The best approach for The Elephant and the southern peaks is from the small settlement of South Kinangop (also called Njabini) which is most easily reached from the main Nairobi - Naivasha road. The roads are tarred to South Kinangop.

It is also possible to enter the national park from the western side of the Aberdare Range. Dirt roads lead from Naivasha, via North Kinangop, up the steep escarpment (and a short section of tar) to Mutubio Gate.

For walkers without their own transport, buses and shared taxis run regularly from Nairobi to Nyeri or Naivasha. From Nyeri, no public transport enters the national park. Hitching a ride is difficult and, as most visitors are likely to be game-viewing in the Salient, lifts up to the moorland are very unlikely. From Naivasha matatus run to South Kinangop and from here walkers can reach the southern peaks.

The routes

The routes included in this section are usually done separately, although it is possible to link the peaks described with others on the range, and follow the entire length of the main ridge of the Aberdares. Guides are essential and vehicle support is recommended. Other logistical requirements mean that visitors with limited time are unlikely to take this option. However, two Nairobi companies can arrange walking safaris in the Aberdares; for more details contact Bushbuck Adventures and Gametrackers at the addresses shown in the Organized walking tours section on p27.

Maps
The Elephant route is covered by the SK Series Y731 1:50M sheet 120/3 (Kipipiri). Ol Doinyo Lesatima is covered by sheet 134/1 (Kinangop). Between them these maps cover the main peaks in the Aberdare Range.

The Elephant

The Elephant is the southernmost peak of the Aberdare Range. Its name is derived from the shape of its outline which, when viewed from the south, resembles that of an elephant. The name of the peak could also refer to the large numbers of elephants inhabiting the densely forested slopes. Walkers will be unlikely to see anything more than huge footprints, but should be prepared for possible encounters.

The route starts at South Kinangop Forest Station (near the small town of the same name) and passes through conifer plantation, montane forest and thick bamboo. In dry weather the section through the bamboo is not unpleasant, but after rain the trails are very boggy and conditions difficult. Passing through the various vegetation zones is interesting but does mean that views are restricted until the lightly wooded slopes and high open moorland are reached. A compass is essential.

In favourable conditions fit and acclimatized walkers could reach The Elephant and return to the forest station in one day, however it is possible to camp near an abandoned hut 30 minutes below the peak, and spread the walk over two days. The views from the peak, of the surrounding plains, the Rift Valley and Mount Kenya, are best in the early morning.

The route keeps to ridges and there is no reliable water source between the forest station and the summit so all supplies should be carried.

Approach
To reach South Kinangop from Nairobi turn right (north-east) off the new Nairobi - Naivasha road 35km after the junction near Limuru where the

Viewed from the ruined hut: the summit of The Elephant

THE ELEPHANT

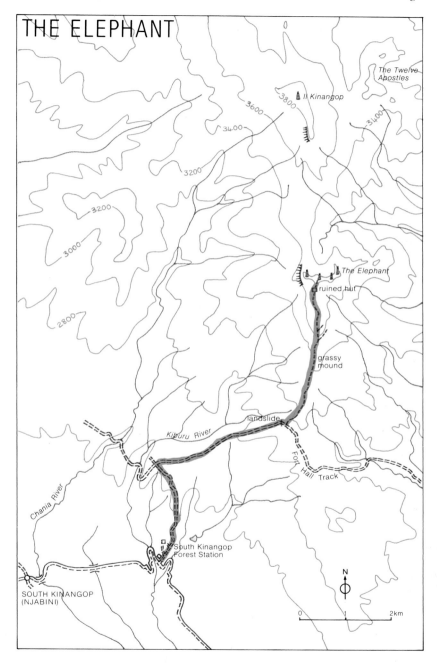

The Twelve
Apostles

Il Kinangop

The Elephant
ruined hut

grassy
mound

landslide

Kiburu River

Fort Hall Track

Chania River

South Kinangop
Forest Station

SOUTH KINANGOP
(NJABINI)

N

0   1   2km

new and old Naivasha roads part. (To turn right it is necessary to turn left then swing round back over the main road on a bridge.) South Kinangop is signposted (24km).

In South Kinangop go straight on, through the town, past the market, and continue on a dirt track, round sharp bends, for 3km. Turn left off the track, by a fire warning sign, into the forest station compound.

At the forest station a sign warns visitors that a permit must be obtained to enter the national park, but this is not usually enforced. Cars may be safely left here and camping is permitted at the rangers' discretion. It may also be possible to arrange for one of the rangers to act as guide or guard if required.

South Kinangop Forest Station to The Elephant Summit
5 - 7 hours 1000m

[1]

0.45

[2]

0.30

[3]

0.40

[4]
0.07
[5]

1.25

[6]

From inside the **forest station [1]** compound a drivable track leads uphill through conifer plantation. Some minor tracks branch off but continue on the highest track to reach a **crossroads [2]**; the track going straight on has been made for logging vehicles and is steep and very rough while the track running left to right is in better condition. (On old maps this crossroads is marked as a T-junction and the main track is called the Fort Hall Track.)

Turn right (north-east) and follow the track uphill. At a clearing fork left to pass pine forest on the right and a steep, bamboo covered hillside dropping down to the left. The track **begins to climb a ridge [3]** and there are valleys on both sides. The track then follows the right side of the ridge and enters dense bamboo; to the left is a steep slope and a low (2m) vertical embankment; to the right the valley side drops away sharply.

Scramble over a small **landslide [4]** that has blocked the track. It may be cleared but this is unlikely. (Determined drivers could reach this point with powerful four-wheel drive, but there is no room to turn round.) Follow the track as it rises then drops slightly. The low embankment on the left ends at this point and a small, steep grassy **clearing [5]** opens out to the left of the track.

A path climbs steeply through long grass and brambles to the top of the clearing then becomes very indistinct as it enters the bamboo and subdivides into numerous game trails. Keep aiming north, up the ridge, avoiding valleys on either side to reach a large **grassy mound [6]**. The main ridge can be seen leading to the top and the square tower of the hut is just visible above the trees.

From the mound the path trends right slightly, then trends

back left to climb the edge of the ridge. Keep aiming north and avoid following game trails that lead rightwards along the side of the hill. Half-way up this ridge the bamboo belt ends and the steep rocky path is easier to follow leading directly to the ruined **hut [7]**.

The four peaks of The Elephant can be clearly seen from the hut. The path keeps to the ridge aiming for the highest peak, second from the left (west), drops to a small col, then climbs steeply up to the **summit [8]** (3590m).

The peak itself is partially covered in small trees but it is possible to see north to the three dome-shaped outcrops that mark the peak of Kinangop, the next main peak of the Aberdare Range, and to a rocky ridge of outcrops further to the right (east) called The Twelve Apostles. The view of Mount Kenya is obscured by the two other peaks of The Elephant to the east, but it can be seen from the hut. To the south and west the hills drop to the Kinangop Plateau and the Rift Valley beyond. The peak of Longonot is also visible.

A path links the summit of The Elephant with its other peaks. It is also possible to reach the summit of Kinangop (3900m) by descending into the large col between The Elephant and Kinangop and then aiming directly towards the summit. A compass is essential in case of mist and this route should not be attempted unless weather conditions are favourable. From the hut to the summit of Kinangop and back to the hut is 5 - 7 hours.

Alternative descent routes from the Elephant Summit are very difficult to find; walkers are advised to retrace their ascent route. From the summit to the hut is 30 minutes, and from the hut to the grassy mound a further 1 - 1$^{1}/_{2}$ hours. The track is reached after 1 - 1$^{1}/_{2}$ hours and the forest station after a further 1$^{1}/_{2}$ - 2 hours. Total time for the descent; 4 - 5$^{1}/_{2}$ hours.

Ol Doinyo Lesatima

Ol Doinyo Lesatima (often shortened to Satima) lies at the northern end of the Aberdare Range. The route to the summit starts at the roadhead of the Wanderis track, which leads through the forested section of the park up onto the open moorland.

In favourable conditions fit and acclimatized walkers can reach the summit of Satima and return to the roadhead in 4 - 6 hours. To drive from Mweiga to the Wanderis track roadhead takes about two hours. Four-wheel drive is recommended and essential for the final section of the track.

The route is within the national park boundary and walkers are required to be accompanied by a park ranger (details in Special conditions on p128).

There are two huts near the top of the Wanderis track and places where camping is possible. Cars can be left at the roadhead. Water is difficult to

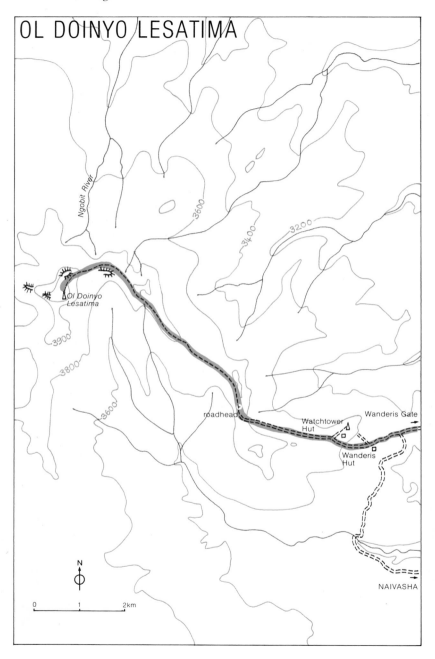

OL DOINYO LESATIMA

Ngobit River

3600

3400

3200

Ol Doinyo
Lesatima

3900

3800

3600

roadhead

Watchtower
Hut

Wanderis Gate

Wanderis
Hut

N

0   1   2km

NAIVASHA

find on the high moorlands and all supplies should be carried.
Nyeri, the nearest town, has shops, a large market, and a range of
hotels and lodging houses suitable for all budgets.

Approach
From the park HQ at Mweiga (10km north of Nyeri) continue north on
the main tarred road for 5km, through Mweiga centre, to turn left onto a
dirt road signposted Enderasha. Follow national park signs, through
farmland, to reach Wanderis Gate after 18km. Enter the park and after
12km fork right (the left fork is signposted to Naivasha). Continue gaining
height through the forest for 1km to reach Wanderis Hut (poor condition)
and a fork. Take the left fork onto a steep narrow track. After 1.5km reach
a junction: turn right to reach Watchtower Hut after 0.5km (basic but
usable, room for 4 people); turn left to reach the roadhead, after 2km, on
the crest of a broad ridge, overlooking the Honi Valley, below and to the
right (south) of a domed rock buttress. Camping is possible here but is
more sheltered near Watchtower Hut. Water is not easily available at
either camping place.
Wanderis is also written Wanderi's, but the apostrophe is generally
dropped.

Wanderis Roadhead to Satima Summit
2 - 3 hours 400m approx.

---

[1]

1.45

[2]

0.15

[3]

0.30

[4]

From the **roadhead [1]** the twin summits of Satima, separated
by a dipped plateau, are visible to the north-west, to the left of
the head of the Honi Valley. The southern summit is the
highest although the exposed grey rock buttress of the
northern summit may appear higher. The path aims
northwards on the left side of a large ridge, indistinct in
places, below the rocky outcrops on the crest of the ridge, to
trend left (north-west) round the head of the Honi Valley to
aim directly towards Satima. Pass to the right of a large
mound on the **broad col [2]** between the head of the Honi
Valley and Ngobit Valley (another large valley to the
right/north) before climbing steeply up towards the summit.
The path continues to trend left below grey **cliffs [3]** and
grassy platforms on the eastern edge of the north summit then
climbs gradually to the mid-point of the dipped plateau,
trending left slightly to reach a large cairn marking the
southern **summit [4]** (4000m).
(Alternatively, scramble up two wide gullies to reach the
northern summit then cross the dipped plateau to reach the
southern summit.)

Descend by the same route; 2 - 2^1/$_2$ hours.

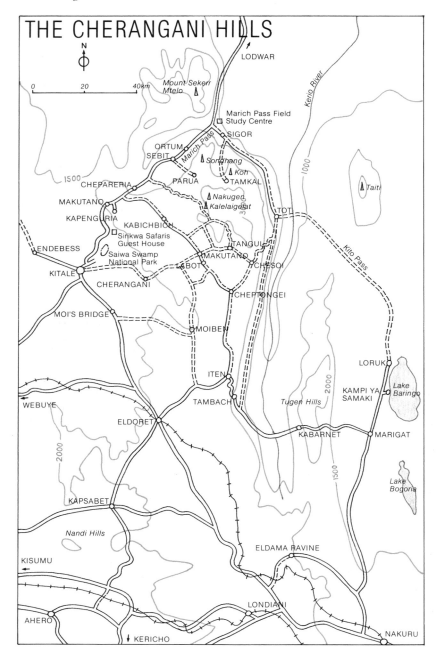

THE CHERANGANI HILLS

The Cherangani Hills

The Cherangani Hills are something of a misnoma. The highest point of the massif, Nakugen, at 3370m/11,055ft is the fourth highest summit in Kenya, and a number of neighbouring peaks rise to over 3000m, making the Cheranganis a mountain range of some significance.

The soil and weather conditions in the Cherangani Hills are favourable so much of the region, especially the lower slopes, is farmland. However, the higher peaks, mainly in the north, have been only lightly settled and make a fine area for walking and backpacking. Walkers in the High Cheranganis can enjoy good views, clear skies, rolling grassland and open moor without any of the remoteness, access difficulties or large wild animals encountered in some of Kenya's other mountain and highland regions.

While most of the high mountains of Kenya (and East Africa) are a result of relatively recent volcanic action, the Cherangani Hills are formed from much older rock, part of an ancient plateau split by the Great Rift Valley. The eastern edge of the Cheranganis is also the western wall of the Rift; one of the steepest and highest of all its escarpments.

The Cheranganis are inhabited mainly by the Marakwet and Pokot peoples (part of the Kalenjin group), living on independent shambas or grouped together in small centres. Before independence the northern hills were part of the 'closed district' of West Pokot, a remote and barely accessible area. Even today many Kenyans, particularly the city dwellers, still regard the Cheranganis as a backward or even dangerous place. These impressions may be reinforced by the fact that many Pokot people continue to dress in their traditional manner; men are frequently seen with large brass earrings and lip-plugs, while women wear neck-rings of beads and headbands decorated with feathers.

In the early 1970s the West Pokot district was designated as suitable for a Special Rural Development Programme. Roads and social amenities were improved and new farming methods encouraged. Kapenguria was developed as the district's administrative headquarters, while nearby Mukatano became the main economic centre.

This local development also has advantages for walkers; communications for drivers and those using public transport are good and approach routes are straightforward. This, combined with the other factors outlined above, make the Cherangani Hills some of the finest walking country in Kenya.

Best time to visit
The wet season in the Cheranganis is generally April-September, and the period before the rains, January-March, is dry but can sometimes be humid. During October, although the rains have ended, some of the smaller tracks may be impassable due to rain damage, but a local road

Dale-country in The Cheranganis: between Kapsangar and Sina

maintenance scheme means repairs are often made quickly. The ideal time to visit is November-December.

Special conditions
Although it is possible for walkers to cover long distances without encountering other people, the Cheranganis are more densely populated than the other high mountain ranges covered in this book. The local people see few foreign tourists but most are friendly and will welcome visitors with interest. Camping near houses or settlements will generally be acceptable but it is more polite and safer to ask permission first from either the landowner or village headman.

Warnings
The pleasant landscape can make the Cheranganis appear deceptively easy. Walkers should not forget that conditions here can be as severe as on Mount Elgon or the Aberdares. Be prepared for heavy rain, cold winds and thick mists on the higher peaks, and do not attempt to do too much without properly acclimatizing.

Approaches
The Cherangani Hills are to the north-east of the large town of Kitale, about 300km north-west of Nairobi. The easiest approach route from Nairobi is on the main tarred road via Nakuru, Eldoret and Kitale to Makutano (near Kapenguria). Beyond Makutano various smaller roads branch off the main road leading to the southern and western Cheranganis. It is also possible to continue on the main road to the Marich Pass and approach the northern Hills from there. Petrol is not available beyond Makutano. For walkers relying on public transport, buses and matatus run regularly between Nairobi, Kitale and Makutano, and (with less frequency) from Makutano into this part of the Cheranganis.

It is also possible to approach the eastern and northern Cheranganis from the east by driving from Nakuru via Marigat to Tot, at the northern end of the Kerio Valley. This road is tarred only as far as Loruk (near Lake Baringo) and petrol cannot be reliably found beyond Nakuru. The road is rough through the Kito Pass. There is no public transport on this road beyond Kampi Ya Samaki and very little traffic.

Once in the Cherangani region several roads lead through the Hills themselves. A good dirt road, called the Cherangani Highway, cuts across the south-western edge of the Hills from near Makutano through Kabichbich, Labot and Cheptongei to Iten, on the Eldoret - Marigat road. A network of smaller tracks called Rural Access Roads (RARs) has been developed, to assist the farmers in this region, which generally lead off the Cherangani Highway to some of the higher, less populated, areas. Cars with four-wheel drive are recommended for the Cherangani Highway and essential for some of the RARs.

Public transport along the Cherangani Highway is limited to occasional matatus linking Makutano with some of the lower settlements on the western side of the Hills, and linking Iten with those on the southern and eastern sides. Walking from one matatu terminus to the other takes two or three days and allows walkers without their own transport to visit some of the peaks in the High Cherangani without having to backtrack on any of their approach routes. Where the roads are steep or in bad condition, or in the less populated areas, no public transport exists although hitch-hikers may be lucky and get a ride with a vehicle serving a police post or mission.

Accommodation

The Cheranganis are not on any of the main tourist circuits and so accommodation of any kind is rather limited.

For walkers visiting the southern part of the Cheranganis, Sirikwa Safaris Guest House is an old settler farmhouse situated amongst forest and farmland just off the main road 26km north of Kitale and 11km south of Makutano. Mrs Barnley and her staff are very welcoming, and can advise on places to visit in the surrounding area. Very knowledgeable bird-guides can also be arranged. Enquiries and bookings to Mrs J Barnley, PO Box 332, Kitale, or to Let's Go Travel, Nairobi (d 1,400/- fb, 840/- bb, c 50/-, 1990).

In the small centre of Kabichbich, on the Cherangani Highway 35km from Makutano, the government rest house is also open to visitors for a nominal charge. This is a simple but well-maintained cabin near the escarpment edge with fine views of Mount Elgon and the surrounding plains. The rest house key is held at the chief's office, but written permission needs to be granted by the District Commissioner in Kapenguria. This should be a straightforward process but the D.C. is often hard to locate.

On the northern side of the Cheranganis is the Marich Pass Field Studies Centre, primarily established as an educational centre for Kenyan

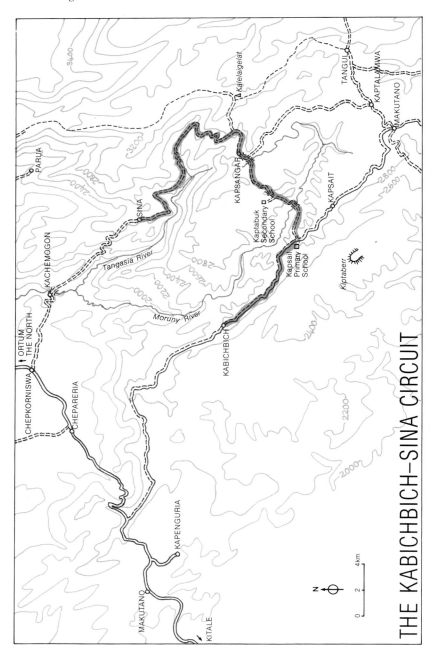

THE KABICHBICH–SINA CIRCUIT

students, but also offering banda accommodation and a campsite for travellers and walkers. To reach the Field Centre from Makutano, continue on the main road for 72km, past the Sigor and Tot road on the right, then after a further 2km turn right onto a dirt road (signposted) to reach the Field Centre after a further 1km. Guides and guards can be arranged or excursions arranged, ranging from short bird-watching walks around the nearby forest and river, through long treks on Mount Sekerr, to vehicle assisted safaris to the dry and rugged South Turkana National Reserve. Enquiries to Mr David Roden, PO Box 2454, Eldoret, Tel (0321) 31541 or Nairobi 332067 (b 70/-, c 40/- 1990).

The routes
The Cheranganis are suitable for walkers of all standards travelling with, or without, their own vehicle. The longer routes, which involve traverses or circular walks, are best approached using public transport as this avoids leaving a vehicle unattended and makes backtracking unnecessary.

Some of the walks described follow drivable, though little used, tracks which can also be followed by visitors with their own car. The routes pass through dramatic and picturesque scenery which is worth visiting (even if viewed from a car) and there are various places where a vehicle can be left and short strolls or day-hikes taken.

For groups travelling together it is sometimes necessary to arrange for one person to drive the car while the others are walking, allowing different drop-off and pick-up points. For those with limited time this method can also reduce overall walking distances.

Cars can sometimes be safely left at police posts, or a local person can be employed to guard the vehicle. Those familiar with African ways will be able to do this, without difficulty, in virtually any town or settlement. Alternatively, guards and/or guides can be arranged through the Marich Pass Field Centre and Sirikwa Safaris Guest House.

Maps
The whole Cherangani area is covered by the SK Series Y503 1:250M sheet NA-36-12 (Kapenguria) (which also includes the main peak area and eastern approaches to Mount Elgon). The Kabichbich - Sina Route is covered by the SK Series Y731 1:50M sheets 75/2 (Sigor) and 75/4 (Cherangani). Sheet 75/2 also covers the Sondhang Circuit and the western approaches to Koh. The dividing line between sheets 75/2 and 76/1 (Chesegon) runs through the summit of Koh and orientation is easier with both maps.

The Kabichbich - Sina Circuit

This route passes through some of the Cheranganis' most beautiful and spectacular scenery, ranging from green and pleasant dale-country to high and imposing escarpments, from lush farmland to harsh semi-desert.

The route begins at the small centre of Kabichbich (pronounced Ky

B'Bich with the emphasis on the first syllable, and also spelt Kaibichbich and Kaipichpich), 35km from Mukatano, and ends at Sina, another small centre, 27km to the east of the main Kitale - Lodwar road. From Kabichbich to Sina is over 40km, which takes 2 - 3 days walking. The distance may appear long but the route follows well maintained, though little frequented, tracks and the walking is not strenuous.

Approach
Follow the main tarred road north from Mukatano, past the road on the right to Kapenguria. After 5km turn right onto the Cherangani Highway dirt road to reach Kabichbich (signposted) after a further 26km. Four-wheel drive and high clearance vehicles are recommended.

As the route begins and ends in different places it is also suitable for walkers using public transport. Matatus run from Mukatano and Cheporaria to Kabichbich, and a pick-up van runs most days between Sina and Cheporaria.

The route passes through the small centre of Kapsangar, which has a duka and hoteli, but there are no other settlememts, although walkers will pass shambas and small groups of huts. Several streams are crossed and camping is possible in a number of places.

Kabichbich to Kapsangar
6 - 8 hours 24km

---

[1] | 3.00 | **[2]** | 0.50 | **[3]** 0.30 **[4]** | 1.20 | **[5]** 0.30 **[6]**	From **Kabichbich [1]** follow the Cherangani Highway in a south-west direction through farmland and wooded areas. After 5km the view to the right (south) opens out and the rocky buttress of Kiptaberr can be seen above the trees about 5km to the south-east. Pass a junction on the left, signposted Imonpochet Primary School, and continue on the main track to reach **Kapsait Primary School [2]**. Turn left 100m after the school onto a RAR, signposted to Kaptabuck Secondary School, which drops downhill through well-kept farmland to ford a small stream, then cross a larger stream on a **bridge [3]**. Continue on the RAR. At a **fork [4]** (the left turn goes to Kaptabuck School) keep right to cross two more bridges. Just after the **second bridge [5]** another track joins from the right. The track continues, crossing another bridge, and climbs up to **Kapsangar [6]** centre.

As the track approaches Kapsangar a row of four conical peaks is visible to the right (east). The highest of these, on the far right, is Kalelaigelat.

It is possible to camp near Kapsangar, with permission, or at one of the pleasant spots near the streams crossed on the approach.

Kapsangar to Sina
4 - 6 hours 20km

[1] 1.00 [2] 4.30 [3]	From **Kapsangar [1]** follow the RAR uphill towards the crest of a broad ridge. In a **small clump of trees [2]**, a track on the right leaves the RAR and climbs up to Kalelaigelat summit, one of the highest peaks in the area, which offers excellent views of the surrounding area, but adds an extra $1^1/2$ - 2 hours to the walk. This is also a good camping place; water is available from the stream in the valley to the right of the track between Kapsangar and the point where the track turns north and starts to climb. Keep on the main track as it crosses the ridge then drops downhill and past a small quarry on the right. This track then winds its way round the heads of several small valleys, fording small streams, passing initially through forest before breaking out into smooth rolling down-country. The valley sides become steeper and the track frequently changes direction but it gradually loses height, eventually running along the right (north-west) side of the large Tangasia Valley, to reach **Sina [3]**.

Sina is a relatively new settlement, established as a result of the new rural development programmes in the area. Tea and basic supplies are available from the duka and hotelis. Camping is possible near the village, with permission, or on one of many suitable places off the RAR before or after Sina.

Camping is also possible, although there is no water, about 3km beyond Sina where the track begins to drop down the escarpment. The views over the plains far below, and beyond to the peaks of Elgon and Dabasien (in Uganda), are among the most spectacular in Kenya, especially at sunset.

Sina - Chepkoniswo

From Sina a local pick-up van runs three to five times each week to Cheporaria, transporting local people and their goods. Walkers preferring not to wait for transport from Sina should be prepared for an extra one or two days' walking.

The track from Sina keeps to the top of the ridge for 3km before zig-zagging down the escarpment, through a series of hairpin bends, onto the plains below. Several footpaths drop directly down the steep escarpment, cutting off the loops, but these can be tiring to follow, especially with a large rucksack. Although the drivable track is longer, the gradient provides easier walking.

The drivable track reaches the main Kitale - Lodwar tarred road at Chepkoniswo, 6.5km north of Cheporaria. From Sina to Cheporaria is

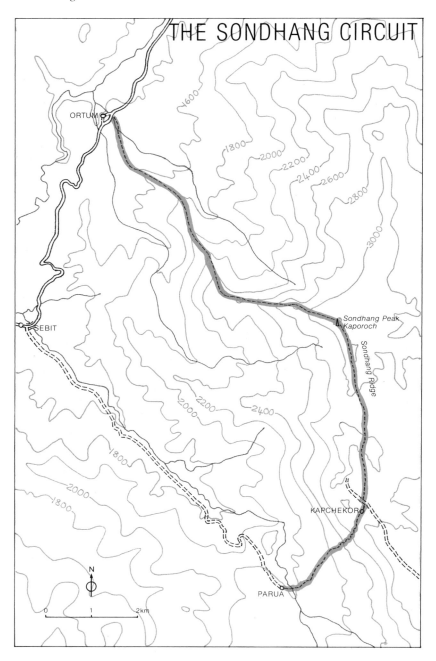

THE SONDHANG CIRCUIT

ORTUM

SEBIT

Sondhang Peak
Kaporoch

Sondhang Ridge

KAPCHEKORO

PARUA

N

0   1   2km

27km and, although the first section of the track leads downhill through woodland, the second section crosses a dry, sparsely-vegetated plain. Water is only reliably found at Kachemogon centre, where the track crosses the Tangasia River.

From Chepkoniswo, public transport runs south to Makutano and Kitale or north to Sebit, Sigor and Lodwar.

The Sondhang Circuit

This route begins by following a RAR but soon leaves the drivable tracks behind to climb the steep western escarpment of the Cheranganis and follow footpaths across open grassland. The route includes Sondhang Peak, the highest point on the large Sondhang Ridge that juts out to the north-west from the main Cherangani plateau.

Approach

The route begins at the small centre of Sebit, on the main Kitale - Lodwar road 45km north of Mukatano, and ends at Ortum, a slightly larger settlement, also on the main road, about 6km north of Sebit. This route, via Parua centre and the crest of the Sondhang Ridge, is 27km and, although it could be done in one day, walkers are advised to take two, breaking the journey at Parua or on the Sondhang Ridge. If leaving a vehicle at one of the centres the total circuit is 33km.

As Sebit and Ortum are both on the main road access is straightforward. A car could be left at either centre by asking a local shopkeeper. Ortum also has a police post where cars could be left.

Matatus and buses run north from Mukatano (three or four per day) stopping at Sebit and Ortum. Although the road is good, traffic is light, and hitching would require patience.

Parua has a duka and hoteli, and camping is possible with permission. The Sondhang Ridge also has several good camping places; water is available from streams but the small settlements on the ridge do not have facilities of any kind.

Although this route can be done in reverse this is not advisable as all the height gain is covered in one very long and steep section.

Sebit to Parua
3 - 4 hours 10km

From **Sebit [1]** a drivable track turns right (south-east) off the main road, signposted to Parua, and leads up a narrow valley. The peak of Sondhang can be seen up and to the left (west). A **primary school [2]** and football field are passed on the left and the track becomes steep and rocky in places. Continue to gain height as the track twists round hairpin bends to reach an area of level ground and **Parua [3]** centre.

Parua to The Ridgetop
2 - 3 hours

From Parua the steep grey cliffs on the main ridge are clearly visible. To the right of these cliffs are two steep broad spurs with a wooded valley in between. The path leads up the spur to the right of the wooded valley towards the lowest point on the skyline at the top of the ridge, crossing several patches of exposed white soil. (See photo.)

[1]
|
1.00
|
[2]
|
1.30
|
[3]
0.10
[4]

From the dukas at **Parua [1]** follow a path leading slightly downhill to the right of the football field. The path up to the foot of the spur does not take a direct line but winds through fields and shambas, crossing three streams on stepping stones, and numerous barbed-wire fences on crude stiles. The path climbs steeply up the spur passing occasional huts and crossing small irrigation channels until the hillside becomes **too steep for cultivation [2]** and the path zig-zags through light bush and crosses patches of exposed white chalky soil. The path enters forest, which becomes increasingly dense as height is gained, until it suddenly ends, just before the crest of the ridge, and the path levels out onto **open grassland [3]**. To the right (south) is the small settlement of **Kapchekor [4]**.

Viewed from Parua: the path aims for the low point on skyline

The Ridgetop to Sondhang Peak Summit
1¹/2 - 2¹/2 hours

Beyond **Kapchekor [1]**, on the highest point of the main ridge, a well-maintained tractor track runs almost due north towards the prominent rocky peak of Sondhang which is visible at the end of the ridge. (The local name for this peak is Koporoch, and the entire ridge is called Sondhang.) There is no single path leading directly to Sondhang Peak but the summit is clearly visible and the way aims directly north, deviating only slightly at various points to skirt fields, avoid boggy sections, or contour round small knolls.

A small square tin-roofed **school [2]** is passed on the right (nearby is the Chelimo Hoteli where tea might be available). The way continues to aim north, over stiles or through gaps in fences, keeping to the high ground and avoiding the heads of steep wooded valleys on either side, to contour round a large knoll and drop slightly to a small col before climbing a steep, rocky, but clearly visible path up to the summit of **Sondhang Peak [3]**.

Sondhang Peak to Ortum
3 - 4 hours

From the **summit [1]** a long ridge points due west then north-west leading down to Ortum centre visible on the valley floor below. It is important to make a careful note of the descent route from this vantage point. As the path descends the view becomes less clear and the many ridges can be confusing. Some sections of the path down from the summit are indistinct and the ridge is intimidatingly steep in places involving easy, but exposed, scrambling. Keep to the ridge at all times even if the way looks difficult or non-existent.

After **turning north-west [2]** the ridge drops in a series of large steps, the path becoming alternately steep then flat, passing huts and compounds, then through fields, before dropping down to cross one final steep section and reach **Ortum [3]**.

Koh

Koh is one of the Cheranganis' most northerly peaks. Unlike the rolling grassland around Kapsangar and Sondhang the landscape is harsher and more rugged; the route up this peak is steep and dramatically exposed at its upper sections. Views from the rocky domed summit of the other peaks in the High Cherangani and down to the semi-desert plains of

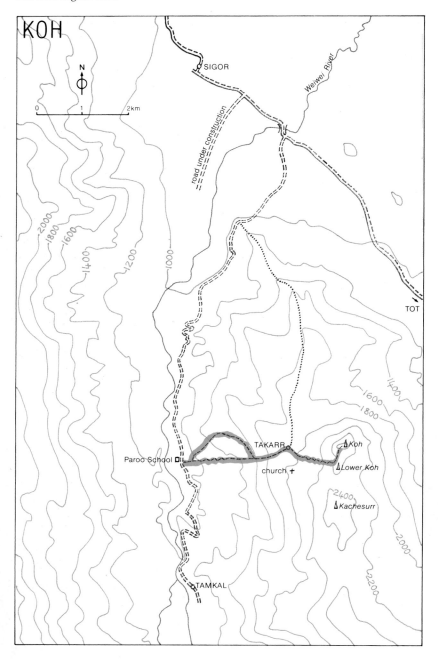

KOH

N

0   1   2km

SIGOR

road under construction

Weiwei River

TOT

TAKARR

△Koh

Paroo School

△Lower Koh

church +

△Kachesurr

TAMKAL

Turkanaland, are among the most impressive in the whole Cherangani range.

Approach

This route begins and ends at Paroo, a primary school and group of huts, 15km from the small town of Sigor, on the northern side of the Cheranganis.

To reach Sigor by car, drive north from Mukatano on the main road towards Lodwar for 70km, through the Marich Pass, to turn right (south-east), over a bridge, and follow the minor road to reach Sigor centre (signposted) after 8km. Buses running between Kitale and Lodwar will drop you at the Sigor turn-off, from where occasional matatus go to Sigor centre, although it might be quicker to walk this last section.

From Sigor to Paroo is a further 14km up the east side of the Weiwei Valley (30 minutes' drive or 3 - 4 hours' walk). From Sigor's main street, which has a market and several dukas, continue on the main dirt road in a south-easterly direction for 2.5km, ignoring the tracks on the right that lead to the post office and up the western side of the Weiwei Valley, to reach a large concrete bridge crossing the river. Immediately after the bridge turn right onto a track that leads towards Tamkal centre and follow this for 11.5km to reach Paroo. This is an interesting approach, passing through vegetated river valley and semi-desert scrub as the track climbs gradually away from the river. Up and to the left the huge smooth rock dome of Koh dominates the head of the valley.

The walk from Paroo to the summit of Koh and back can easily be done in a day. An early start is advised, so that most of the route is covered

Koh summit from Takarr　　　　　　　　　　　　　　　　　*Sondhang Ridge*

while the western side of the mountain is still in the shade. Camping, with permission, is possible near the school, or at several other points between the river and the track beyond Paroo.

The path from Paroo up to the summit subdivides in many places and can cause confusion. A guide is recommended. This can be arranged through the Marich Pass Field Studies Centre (see Accommodation), or occasionally through the school. Boys from the surounding settlements stay at the school, returning home at weekends, so it may be easier to find a guide to show you the way to the summit on Friday or Saturday.

Paroo to Koh Summit
4 - 5 hours

From **Paroo school [1]** the smooth, domed summit of Koh, with a near-vertical north face, can be clearly seen to the east with Lower Koh, a smaller rounded peak, to its right (south). Walk through a flat area of land opposite the school and cross a stream on stepping stones. Numerous paths lead up to a small settlement on the mountain called Takarr. If you do not have a guide take a compass bearing on the summit and aim straight up the steepest section of the valley side to reach the flatter area around the small scattered settlement of **Takarr [2]**. Alternatively, for a less steep approach, climb the ridge to the left (north) of the flat area opposite the school and follow one of the many paths that climb to its crest. The main path passes through thick bush and initially aims in a northerly direction before swinging round north-east, then east, then finally south, keeping below and to the right of the main ridge that leads up to Takarr. The Weiwei Valley and Paroo school are visible below and to the right. Koh is up to the left but the view is blocked by the dense vegetation. At this point, near a small group of huts, this path is joined by other paths leading straight up from Paroo. Follow the steepest path, still through dense bush, to reach Takarr. (The path passes the occasional hut, with small patches of maize or goat pens and it may be possible to check directions with local people.)

From Takarr, Koh and Lower Koh are clearly visible, (the third peak, standing apart and to the right of the Koh peaks is called Kachesurr). Paths lead out of **Takarr [3]** towards Lower Koh. Keep trending right as the path gains height, aiming towards Kachesurr for some sections, until the path crosses a wide (15m) **strip of bare rock [4]**, and continues to zig-zag up, crossing and recrossing the bare strip.

Continue trending right up to the right end of the steep cliffs of Lower Koh. The path then turns left (north) and runs along the base of these **cliffs [5]**, which are a pink-orange colour,

[1]

1.30

[2]
[3]

0.30

[4]

0.20

[5]
0.10
[6]

|
0.30

[7]

streaked with black, and overhanging in places. To the left the valley side drops away steeply. The path trends right, to enter a wooded valley, at the top of which is the **col [6]** separating Lower Koh from the main peak.

From the col, scramble up the steep, rocky, and sparsely vegetated mountainside to reach the **summit of Koh [7]**.

On the way up, trend left to reach the sloping rock shelves for spectacularly exposed views of the Weiwei Valley. From the summit it is possible to see down to Sigor and the plains beyond, crossed by a perfectly straight line of pylons carrying electricity from the Turkwell Gorge, hidden behind the peaks of the Sekerr massif. To the east the plains extend to the foot of the Kerio Valley with the peak of Taiti (a northern extension of the Tugen Hills) beyond. To the south, beyond the summit of Lower Koh, a large ridge leads through the Lelan Forest to the central peaks of the High Cherangani.

To descend, retrace the path to Takarr. A useful landmark is the church, the only large square tin-roofed building in the settlement, on the end of a short spur. To the right (north) is another spur and the way down keeps to this second spur. From Takarr the easiest and most direct route to Paroo is straight down, on any of the numerous paths. The school is visible from clearings in the dense bush to act as a landmark. From the summit to Paroo is 2 - 3 hours.

All enquiries welcomed:

KENYA
Bushbuck Safaris
Gilfillan House
Kenyatta Avenue
PO Box 67449
Nairobi, Kenya
Tel 729639, 521554
Tlx 25517 DIVADVICE
Fax 728737

EUROPE
Wildlife Safaris
26 Newnham Green
Maldon, Essex CM9 6HZ
Great Britain
Tel (0621) 853172
Fax 081 599 0772

USA
Safari Centre International
(ref: Bushbuck Adventures)
Toll Free 800 6245342

'A peg above the rest!'

Let us organise a safari to suit your requirements
OR
Choose from our exciting Adventure itineraries that depart on a regular basis. Take ADVANTAGE of:- Our experienced guide and naturalist who accompanies each adventure - Small group sizes - Flexibility - Comfortable Camps - Showers - Excellent camp cuisine - The chance to get out and walk - Visit places that others only dream about:- Masai Mara - Lake Victoria - Mt. Elgon - Saiwa Swamp - Chyulu Hills - Kenya Coast - Mt. Kenya - Mathews Range - Lake Turkana - and many more places.

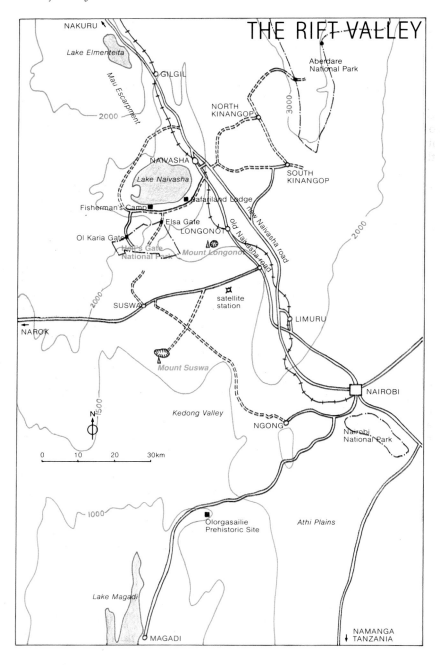

The Rift Valley Mountains

According to the theory of plate tectonics, the land masses of Africa and Arabia are slowly moving apart. This has resulted in the creation of the Great Rift Valley, a huge fault in the earth's surface which runs the length of Africa, for over 4000km, from the Red Sea to Mozambique. For some of its distance the Rift Valley divides into two and the eastern branch passes through Kenya.

The mountains of Longonot and Suswa, and the gorge of Hell's Gate, are all in the Rift Valley, to the north-west of Nairobi, and offer a fascinating selection of walking routes which include volcanic craters, hot springs, steam vents, caves, cliffs, rock towers and superb views of the surrounding lakes and plains.

Mount Longonot and Mount Suswa are best viewed from the new Nairobi - Naivasha road, which runs along the top of the eastern Rift Valley escarpment. From the viewpoints Longonot is immediately obvious; a classic volcanic cone, appearing almost perfectly circular at its base with steep sides, scarred by deep gullies, rising to the rim of a crater and series of jagged peaks. The circular walk around the rim of the crater (more correctly called the caldera) is dramatic and exhilarating.

Mount Suswa lies to the south-west of Mount Longonot (to the left when seen from the escarpment viewpoints) and is also an extinct volcano. Suswa is much larger than Longonot, but its main peaks are lower - its size is deceptive, appearing to be nothing more than a low range of hills. Only inside the main caldera does the extent of Suswa become evident and the mountain take on a completely different appearance. Walkers and drivers can easily ascend the outer side of the mountain to cross the broad crater floor and reach the high peaks overlooking the 'Lost World' of the inner caldera. Suswa also contains a number of large caves which are interesting to explore.

Hell's Gate is a large gorge lying to the north-west of Longonot. From the viewpoints on the new Nairobi - Naivasha road, the tall orange cliffs of the western side of the gorge can be seen amongst the tree-covered hills and plains between Longonot and Lake Naivasha. This gorge and the surrounding area, while not a mountain, is an excellent area for camping and backpacking so some information for walkers has been included in this section.

Best time to visit

The three areas described in this section are easier to reach, and the walking likely to be more enjoyable, during the dry seasons; December to mid-February and May to September. During rainy periods access on the dirt tracks to Suswa is difficult for walkers and vehicles, and on Longonot walkers have to confront torrential streams running down the steep paths to the crater rim. Although it is possible to walk in some parts of Hell's Gate during the rains, the most interesting sections, in the lower gorge, are impossible to reach due to flood water.

Special conditions

Mount Longonot and Hell's Gate have been gazetted as national parks and gates are positioned on the main approach routes where park entrance fees are payable. Entry is not restricted to visitors in vehicles, however, so these parks are ideal for walkers and all tourists relying on public transport or hitch-hiking.

Mount Suswa is not a national park and, although the main approach routes cross private ranchland, access is straightforward.

Warnings

Although access to all the above areas can be difficult in the rainy season, visiting during the dry periods can lead to problems with water supply. There is no water on Mount Longonot and, although the circuit of the crater can easily be done in a day, the climb is steep and conditions often very hot, so walkers should fill their bottles from the tank at the park gate.

On Mount Suswa, Maasai people living in the crater have dug pools to collect rain water, but there are no springs or other water sources. Visitors to Suswa should carry all their water supplies.

In Hell's Gate, water is available from taps at the park gates and at the ranger post and interpretation centre inside the park, but during the dry season there is usually no water in the gorge itself. On the plains beyond the gorge are Maasai *manyattas* (compounds), but the water supply there cannot be relied upon.

There have been occasional reports of security problems on Longonot and Suswa; unattended cars were broken into or tampered with. However, since rangers have been stationed at the foot of Longonot, cars can be safely left and there have been no further reports of any other problems. On Suswa, cars have been safely left for a morning or afternoon but security cannot be certain.

Maps

Longonot and Hell's Gate are covered by SK Series Y731 1:50M sheet 133/4 (Longonot). In the same series, Suswa is covered by sheet 147/2 (Ol Doinyo Onyoke).

Mount Longonot

Mount Longonot is 2777m/9,100ft high, rising some 700m/2,300ft above the floor of the Rift Valley. The caldera is circular with a flat floor, over a kilometre in diameter, with steep-sided walls, up to 350m/1,200ft high below the main peak. The crater floor is covered in vegetation; a secluded habitat for numerous species of animals and birds. Steam jets rise from the floor of the crater which may indicate that Mount Longonot is not completely extinct but merely dormant.

The mountain remains very much as it was when first reached by the explorers Fischer and, later, Thomson in 1883. Thomson's descriptions of the area around Mount Longonot provided inspiration for several novels by J Rider Haggard, creator of swashbuckling hero Alan Quartermain.

Walkers can reach the crater rim of Mount Longonot and look down into the caldera. It is also possible to do a complete circuit of the rim and reach the highest point of the mountain. This is an excellent walk which can easily be completed in a day. No climbing is involved (although some sections of the path are fairly steep) and guides are not required.

Approach

Mount Longonot lies about 60km to the north-west of Nairobi. The nearest settlement is the small centre of Longonot, on the old Nairobi - Naivasha road. To reach Longonot from Nairobi by car there are several possible routes.

The new and old Nairobi - Naivasha roads divide about 30km outside Nairobi, near the town of Limuru. The new road runs along the top of the escarpment. After about 45km, just as this main road begins to descend to Naivasha, a minor dirt road is signposted on the left to Longonot centre. This drops steeply down the escarpment to the valley floor and joins with the old Nairobi - Naivasha road to the north of Longonot centre.

From the junction near Limuru, the old Nairobi - Naivasha road drops down the escarpment to Maai-Maihu (pronounced 'Mai-Mayu'). This road has been damaged by the many lorries using this route and is in very bad condition. Longonot centre is about 10km north of Maai-Maihu.

For those relying on public transport, fast buses and shared taxis run regularly along the new road to Naivasha. From there local matatus run along the old road back to Longonot. Matatus also run along the old road from Nairobi and Limuru via Maai-Mahiu.

Hitching out of Nairobi is difficult. It is easier to take public transport out along the Naivasha road (via Kikuyu or Limuru) as far as the junction where the old and new Nairobi - Naivasha roads divide and hitch from there.

From Longonot centre, the track to the national park gate runs to the west of the railway line. Vehicles must cross the railway at the level crossing on the southern side of the centre. (For vehicles approaching from Maai-Maihu the track turns off the Naivasha road just before the level crossing.)

Buses and matatus stop near the police station, opposite a line of dukas and hotelis, and from here several footpaths lead down to cross the railway and join the track to the park gate.

From Longonot centre to the park gate and ranger station is about 4km or an hour's walk. Cars can be left at the park gate. Camping is permitted and water and toilets are available.

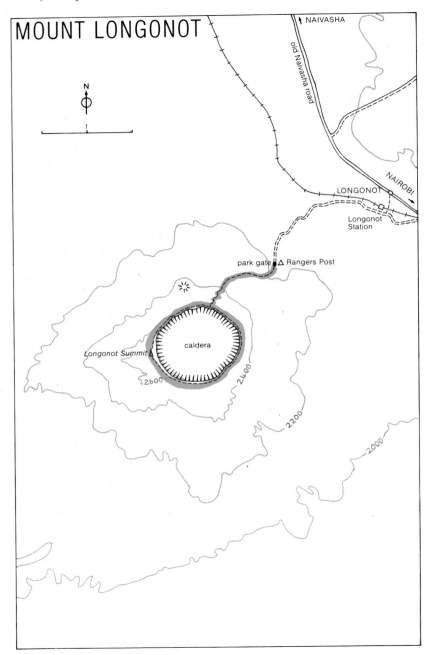

MOUNT LONGONOT

N

NAIVASHA

old Naivasha road

NAIROBI

LONGONOT

Longonot
Station

park gate △ Rangers Post

caldera

Longonot Summit

2600

2400

2200

2000

Park Gate to Longonot Summit and Return
4 - 6¹/2 hours

From the ranger station the drivable track continues for about 300m to a picnic area. Nearby are two thatched 'picnic bandas'. The path up to Longonot turns right off the drivable track here.

The walking is generally easy as the clear path winds round a foothill before climbing up the steep side of the cone itself. Rainwater has made many deep gullies in the soft ash soil and the path has also been eroded in many places. Walkers must sometimes follow the gullies which involves occasional scrambling. Continue to reach the lip (lowest point) of the crater rim, (1 - 2 hours from ranger station).

The panorama from the lip includes the Aberdares (cloud permitting), Lake Naivasha and the Mau Escarpment. At the lip it is also possible to see down into the caldera and across to the high peaks on the south-western side of the mountain.

The path round the crater is clear and easy to follow, although steep in places. Walking in a clockwise direction is easier as the high peaks are climbed earlier and the path then descends gradually back to the lip. From the lip to the summit takes 1 - 1¹/2 hours. On the way round this section of the crater, walkers can see down to Lake Naivasha and Hell's Gate, and also to the small subsidiary cone on Longonot's northern side. To reach the summit involves a steep muddy scramble past the toppled trig point. From the summit, the mass of Suswa rising above the plains of the Kedong Valley, can be seen to the south-west.

From the summit back to the lip is 1¹/2 - 2 hours and the final descent a further 45 minutes.

Mount Suswa

Mount Suswa lacks Longonot's classic conical shape, appearing low and undramatic, but once the rim of Suswa has been reached, the mountain becomes more impressive; the main caldera is much larger than Longonot's and the area inside the crater walls creates an impression of remoteness and isolation. The caldera has a wide, flat, grassy floor and groups of Maasai, living in small manyattas, graze their cattle and goats here.

Suswa's main caldera also contains an inner caldera at its southern side and within this inner caldera is a large steep-sided, flat-topped plateau separated from the main caldera floor by a circular 'moat', which was formed when the surrounding lava was faulted and collapsed. This unusual feature is very difficult to reach; the local Maasai call it the 'Lost World' and, due to its inaccessibility, it remained largely unexplored until as recently as 1980.

Walkers can follow the drivable track up to the crater rim and easily cross the floor of the main caldera to reach the roadhead at the base of the

155

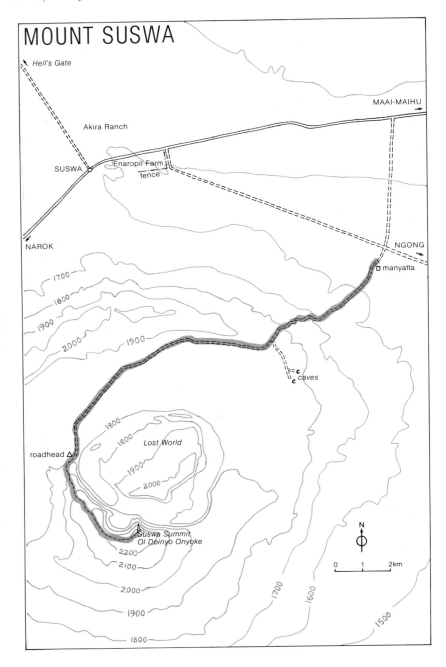

MOUNT SUSWA

Hell's Gate

Akira Ranch

MAAI-MAIHU

SUSWA

Enaropil Farm

fence

NAROK

NGONG

manyatta

1700

1800

1900

2000

1900

caves

1800

1800

Lost World

roadhead

1900

2000

Suswa Summit

Ol Doinyo Onyoke

2200

2100

2000

1900

1800

1700

1600

1500

N

0   1   2km

high peaks. The highest peak of Suswa, at 2360m/7,730 ft, is Ol Doinyo Onyoke (Maasai for 'Red Mountain') which, with vehicle assistance, can be reached in a day and affords excellent views of the Lost World and the calderas.

A series of caves, formed by lava tubes, lie on the eastern side of the main caldera. These are a popular attraction, and properly equipped cavers can explore large systems, while less intrepid visitors can enter the caves as far as their torch and sensibilities will allow.

Approach

Mount Suswa lies about 50km to the north-west of Nairobi and about 25km to the south of Longonot. Drivers can approach on the old Nairobi - Naivasha road via Maai-Maihu (described in the section on Mount Longonot), or on the Kodong Valley road via Ngong.

From Maai-Maihu take the road towards Narok and the Maasai Mara National Reserve. After 11.5km the satellite tracking station is passed. After a further 7.5km a track branches from the tarred road on the left. This is not signposted but leads directly towards Mount Suswa. After 6km this track crosses a wide dirt road (this is the Suswa - Ngong road), then after another 1km leads to a group of manyattas and the start of the track up the mountain.

If you miss the track to the mountain continue on the tarred road towards Suswa centre (30km from Maai-Maihu). Another track branches off on the left 3.2km before Suswa centre, signposted 'Kedong Ranch, Private' . This leads round the boundary of Enaropil Farm to join with the Suswa - Ngong road (dirt) which meets the track described above.

Public transport or hitch-hiking to Maai-Maihu is straightforward (described in the section on Mount Longonot). From Maai-Maihu occasional matatus run towards Narok and can drop you at one of the tracks which branch off the tarred road. No public transport goes to the base of the mountain from this direction. You may get a lift with other visitors (Suswa is a popular weekend destination for people from Nairobi), or on a farm vehicle, but do not rely on this.

The second approach route from Nairobi, via Ngong and the Kedong Valley, is more interesting but is mainly on dirt road which is slower than the approach via Maai-Maihu and may be impassable after the rains. From Nairobi drive through Karen to Ngong town. Turn right in the town then right again at the small traffic circle to follow tarred road for a few kilometres. At a fork the tarred road bears right and the graded dirt road continues straight on, to drop down a series of escarpments towards the Rift Valley floor. From the edge of the final escarpment Suswa and Longonot can be seen. Follow this road past a number of small settlements until the dirt road is passing along the eastern flank of Suswa (i.e. to the left). From Ngong town to the manyattas at the start of the track up the mountain is 58 kilometres. Petrol is not available on this route. No regular public transport passes Suswa on this road. Lorries and farm vehicles do travel this way, but getting a lift right to the foot of Suswa would require a great deal of luck and patience.

The Manyattas to The Roadhead

From the manyattas at the foot of the mountain a rough, but drivable, track leads to the lip (lowest point) of the crater rim. This track is badly eroded in places, particularly at its start where the direction is unclear, and some minor diversions have to be taken to avoid the deep gullies, but it is generally easy to follow. From the manyattas to the crater lip is about 6km and takes about one hour to drive or $1^1/_2$ - 2 hours to walk. One section of this track may be unclear: at a wide rock pan, reached after 3.5km, the route appears to lead straight on, but in fact leaves the pan on its right side before swinging round to the left again to continue up the mountain.

At the lip the track divides: the left branch leads through trees and light bush to the caves; the right branch leads through trees and then across the grassy crater floor in a broad arc, parallel to the inner wall of the main crater, past some manyattas, to reach the roadhead after 11km, 45 minutes' drive or 2 - 3 hours' walk. It is not possible to drive beyond this point. There is an area of level ground here, right on the edge of the inner caldera with excellent views of the route to the summit, which makes a good camping place.

The Roadhead to Suswa Summit
$1^1/_2$ - 2 hours

From the roadhead the path leads round the edge of the inner caldera towards the highest peak. It is easy to follow in most places but is occasionally unclear; if in doubt keep to the left (i.e. towards the edge of the caldera). At the summit is a concrete trig point marked 'DOS 1949, SKP 109, Suswa (Nyukie)' and the remains of a metal gantry which seems to have been used to put the trig point in place.

From the summit of Mount Suswa it is possible to see both the inner and outer calderas and the 'Lost World'. To the north-east is Mount Longonot. Left (west) of Longonot, jets of steam rising from the area around Hell's Gate are visible.

Allow 1 - $1^1/_2$ hours for the return to the roadhead.

The return walk from the roadhead to the manyattas is 4 - 5 hours.

Hell's Gate

Although not a mountain, Hell's Gate has been included in this chapter because the area is excellent for walking. Conditions are not strenuous and access by car and public transport is straightforward.

Hell's Gate National Park lies to the south of Lake Naivasha, a relatively small park, roughly 14km by 5km, containing an area of rolling grassland where numerous animals, including zebra, buffalo and various species of gazelle, can be seen. The main feature of the park, however, is a series of high red-rock cliffs that form a wide gorge. The rock is actually composed lava formed into vertical columnar sections. Geologists believe that many thousands of years ago, the gorge drained a huge lake that covered this part of the Rift Valley floor.

A drivable dirt road leads through the national park and upper gorge to a viewpoint overlooking the lower gorge, which is deep and narrow. After heavy rain the stream in the lower gorge becomes a powerful river, but in dry periods walking is possible here. The lower gorge, which gives the national park its name, is actually outside the park boundary. However, a steep path leads from the upper gorge down to the floor of the lower gorge, and it is here that the scenery is most impressive and the walking most dramatic.

On the hills overlooking the park and in the lower gorge, numerous hot springs and steaming geysers led to the gorge being named Hell's Gate by Dr Fischer, the German naturalist, one of the first Europeans to reach this area. In 1883 he entered the gorge from the south, and his expedition was attacked by Maasai warriors near the rock tower at the head of the upper gorge that now bears his name.

In more recent times a power station has been constructed above the main gorge walls to harness the geothermal energy. Fortunately it cannot be seen from the upper or lower gorge and impressive natural scenery is not spoilt.

Approach

Hell's Gate National Park lies about 70km to the north-west of Nairobi. The nearest town is Naivasha which can be easily reached by car, public transport or hitch-hiking along the new main road from Nairobi that runs along the top of the Rift Valley escarpment. The main road to Naivasha is tarred and in good condition. Naivasha has a petrol station, a market and shops where most supplies can be bought.

From Naivasha drivers should leave the town in a southerly direction, and follow the old road, back towards Nairobi, for 5km to turn right (south-west) onto Moi South Lake Road (signposted). After 3km pass the entrance to the Lake Naivasha Hotel on the right. Continue on the road passing through farmland and flower plantations.

The Elsa Gate entrance to Hell's Gate National Park is signposted on the left after about 16km and reached after about 2km of dirt road. A farther 8km round Moi South Lake Road, a tarred road on the left leads to the geothermal power station and Ol Karia Gate. It is also possible to approach the Lake Road South junction from Maai-Maihu on one of the approach routes described in the Longonot section.

A bus and matatus run two or three times per day from Naivasha around the Lake Road South, and it may be possible to hitch a ride with

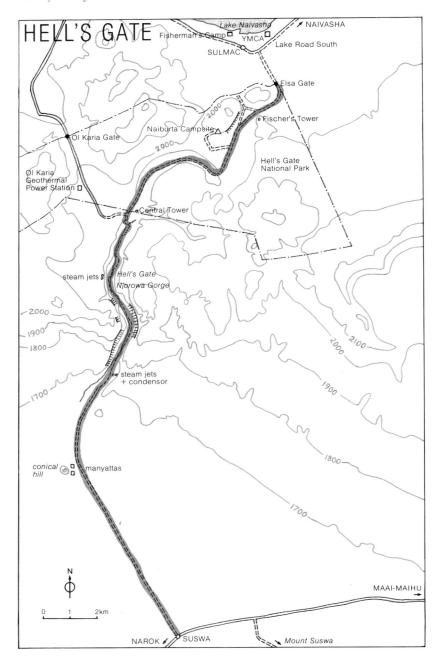

HELL'S GATE

Lake Naivasha → NAIVASHA
Fisherman's Camp □ YMCA □
SULMAC Lake Road South

● Elsa Gate

2000 ● Fischer's Tower

Naiburta Campsite △

● Ol Karia Gate

Hell's Gate
National Park

2000

Ol Karia
Geothermal
Power Station □

● Central Tower

steam jets Hell's Gate
Njorowa Gorge

2000
1900
1800

steam jets
+ condensor

1700

2100
2000

1900

1800

conical ◎ □ manyattas
hill □

1700

N

MAAI-MAIHU →

0   1   2km

NAROK ↙ ● SUSWA ↘ Mount Suswa

160

other tourists or farm vehicles. It is easier for walkers to enter the park at Elsa Gate than at Ol Karia Gate.

Accommodation

Visitors to Lake Naivasha and Hell's Gate have a selection of accommodation to choose from.

At Safariland Lodge, on Lake Road South, 10km from the Lake Road South junction, guests stay in individual cottages, all with bathroom, situated in pleasant grounds by the side of the lake around a central bar and restaurant (d 2,100/- hb 1990). Camping is permitted (100/-). The lodge has a swimming pool, and horse-riding and boating are also available.

A farther 5km along the Lake Road South is the YMCA/Youth Hostel which offers very basic banda accommodation (35/-) and campsite facilities (25/-).

Beyond this, 18km from the Lake Road South junction, and 2km past the Elsa Gate turn-off, is Fisherman's Camp which has bandas (150/-) and a pleasant grassy campsite on the lakeside (40/-). There is also a reasonably priced youth hostel-style dormitory with showers and cooking facilities, but this is closed during November and from January to March. Fisherman's Camp can sometimes provide information leaflets and maps about activities and walks in the area around Lake Naivasha. Boats can be hired free of charge.

Inside the national park, Naiburta Campsite is situated on a small grassy plateau near the high cliffs overlooking the grassy central area of the park. This site has no facilities, but water is available from Elsa Gate or from the ranger station at the southern end of the park. (Camping may also be allowed here, with permission from the rangers on duty.)

Frozen fish, fresh fruit and vegetables are available from the farm next to Fisherman's Camp. Other basic supplies can be bought from the dukas at the Sulmac village in between the Elsa Gate turn-off and Fisherman's Camp.

The routes

Two routes are described here; the first follows the upper gorge and remains within the national park boundary, while the second follows the lower gorge and crosses the plains beyond. The routes can be combined into a two-day walk and can also be done in reverse.

Elsa Gate to Upper Gorge Roadhead
2 - 3 hours 10km

From Elsa Gate a drivable dirt road passes though the central portion of the park and enters the upper gorge. Fischer's Tower, an impressive monolith of rock standing apart from the left wall of the gorge, is obvious. The rocks at the base of the tower are inhabited by a group of rock hyrax, small rodent-like animals related (in zoological terms) to the elephant, which are remarkably tame. A sign warns visitors not to feed them.

At Fischer's Tower the road divides; keep on the main track that continues down the gorge which widens out again on the left into grassy rolling hills where zebra and gazelle can often be seen. On the right side of the road is the main wall, a 400ft sheer cliff, the highest part of the upper gorge, popular with local rock-climbers and home to large flocks of swifts.

The main wall drops in height at its left end and a track branches off on the right, 4km from Elsa Gate, leading up to the campsite. The main track continues down the gorge for a further 6km, past more cliffs, and the ranger station and interpretation centre on the left (with the rocky buttress of Central Tower behind), to reach another fork. The track to the right leads steeply up the side of the gorge past the geothermal power station to Ol Karia Gate and out of the park. The left fork leads to the viewpoint overlooking the lower gorge. A notice board marks the park boundary.

From the right side of the viewpoint a steep path leads down the side of the gorge to the river bed at the bottom. Near the top of this path, sulphurous water issues from a hot spring and runs through an earth channel turned deep green with algae. During the rainy season there is water flowing along the river bed, but (except after heavy rains) it is usually possible to walk along the lower gorge to see the high cliffs, rock towers, hot springs and steam vents.

The narrow, most impressive, section of the lower gorge extends for about 7km from the base of the steep path below the viewpoint. Walkers can leave their tents and equipment at the campsite or ranger post to follow the gorge for a short distance and return to the viewpoint and national park, or continue along the river bed at the bottom of gorge and out onto the plains beyond, eventually to meet the tarred Nairobi - Narok road near Suswa centre.

This is an interesting walk through a variety of landscapes and passing a number of Maasai manyattas on the way. Water supplies on the route are not reliable so walkers should be self-contained.

In dry conditions cars can negotiate the river bed, but it is impossible to drive by car between the upper and lower gorge.

The Lower Gorge to Suswa centre
4 - 7 hours 20km

From the steep path down from the viewpoint follow the river bed downstream as it winds between high cliffs, covered in patches of vegetation, and banks of grey chalky soil. The strata of the main cliffs, in various shades of grey and yellow, is capped by a dark orange layer of rock and top-soil. After the rains these colours are more distinct but in the dry periods they are dull and dusty. The river bed is composed of black gritty soil and chunks of obsidian can be found. The banks of the river are lined with trees and bushes including giant euphorbia candelabras and yellow-trunked acacias. Sections of a metal pipe can also be seen, the remains of a water supply system for the dry ranchland on the plains, since destroyed by powerful flood water.

After 3km a large steam vent can be seen at the foot of the cliffs on the right. It is possible to scramble up to the vent but care should be taken as the rock underfoot is very fragile. After another kilometre, two large rock towers are passed on the right and the gorge begins to open out although the walls are still at least 300ft high. Grey sand and flood debris litters the gorge floor. About 1.5km from the rock towers a drivable track leaves the river bed, crossing it again farther down.

About $1^1/_2$ - 2 hours' walking (6km) from the start of the lower gorge, a prominent block of columnar sections can be seen to the left of the path with clouds of steam issuing from its base. At this point, the local Maasai have built a simple condenser unit out of an oil drum and sections of pipe to collect water droplets formed by cooling steam. The water is conserved in a nearby concrete trough.

The track continues for 3.5km to a group of manyattas at the foot of a prominent flat-topped conical hill which is passed to the left to join a good dirt road that runs southerly, almost straight, across the plains. After about 5km the tin roofs of the buildings in Suswa centre can be seen and reached after another 5km. From Suswa centre the tarred road leads west to Narok and the Maasai Mara, or east back to Maai-Maihu (30km) and the old Nairobi - Naivasha road.

MODEL PWP

personal water purifier

◆ Safe, clean drinking water

◆ Proven by independent tests

◆ Compact and easy to use

◆ Treatment capacity — 500 litres or 5 years

Further information direct from the manufacturers:

Pre-Mac (Kent) Limited,
103 Goods Station Road,
Tunbridge Wells, Kent TN1 2DP.

Telephone: 0892 34361
Fax: 0892 515770

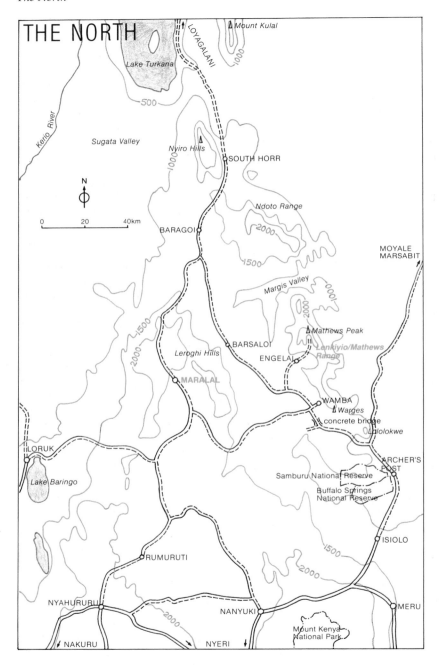

THE NORTH

Mount Kulal
LOYAGALANI
Lake Turkana
Kerio River
Sugata Valley
Nyiro Hills
SOUTH HORR
N
0   20   40km
Ndoto Range
BARAGOI
MOYALE
MARSABIT
Margis Valley
Mathews Peak
BARSALOI
Leroghi Hills
ENGELAI
Lenkiyio/Mathews
Range
MARALAL
WAMBA
Warges
concrete bridge
Ololokwe
ILORUK
ARCHER'S
POST
Samburu National Reserve
Lake Baringo
Buffalo Springs
National Reserve
ISIOLO
RUMURUTI
MERU
NYAHURURU
NANYUKI
Mount Kenya
National Park
NAKURU
NYERI

The North

To the north and west of Mount Kenya, and the fertile farmlands of the Central Highlands, the land drops over a thousand metres (3000 feet) towards the vast semi-desert plains that make up the 'forgotten half' of Kenya. This region is very thinly populated and generally marked by a harsh and inhospitable climate, where daytime temperatures are often over 100°F (28°C) and the average rainfall is less than 10 inches (250mm) per year.

During the colonial era this region was called the Northern Frontier District, and older Kenyans may still refer to it as the 'NFD', but today it falls within the vast Rift Valley, Eastern and North-Eastern Provinces. There are few towns in this region; most of the population are semi-nomadic pastoralists, herding goats, cattle and camels across the sparse landscape between waterholes and grazing grounds.

Rising above this generally hot and barren landscape are several mountains. As the warm air rises to pass these high points it cools, forming clouds, which often result in rain. Consequently these isolated mountains have a good water supply and are well vegetated, able to support a range of wildlife and also providing valuable grazing ground for domestic animals.

The main groups of people found in the north of Kenya include Turkana, Rendille, Boran, Gabbra, Somali, and Samburu, who are closely related to the Maasai, sharing many of their customs and dressing in a similar, highly decorative, manner. Young Samburu men become *morans* (warriors) when aged about sixteen, decorating their hair and faces with red ochre paint and wearing necklaces and earrings of coloured beads. Most morans wear a short red robe and all carry a spear making them striking figures. Samburu women also wear red robes and are frequently adorned with neck-rings, headbands and earrings made from beads.

The Samburu place great value on their cattle; young boys learn about domestic animals by firstly tending goats and after becoming morans they are entrusted with the family's herd, travelling great distances with the cows in search of water or fresh grazing ground. Consequently the morans' knowledge of an area, and the behaviour of wild animals found there, make them valuable guides for walkers in the mountain areas described in this chapter.

Most of these northern mountain ranges would make ideal areas for walking but their remoteness makes access difficult, particularly for visitors with limited time or without their own vehicle. However, two areas which offer excellent walking opportunities, and where access is relatively straightforward, are included in this chapter. Routes are not described step-by-step, as in these areas local guides are recommended, so instead a selection of suggested destinations has been included.

The Lenkiyio/Mathews Range

The mountains of northern Kenya form an extended chain that stretches across the vast semi-desert plains from Mount Kulal in the north, near the southern tip of Lake Turkana, down to Lololokwe in the south, a huge orange buttress with sheer cliff walls, to the north of Isiolo and Samburu National Reserve. The Lenkiyio Hills lie towards the southern end of this chain between Warges, a high solitary peak to the east of the small town of Wamba, and the Ndoto Mountains, the largest of the northern ranges.

The first European to reach this area was the explorer Count Samuel Teleki (who, later in the same expedition, also discovered Lake Turkana), and the range was named by him for General Lloyd Mathews, a commander in the Sultan of Zanzibar's army, who had helped Teleki prepare for the expedition. The hills are still frequently referred to as the Mathews Range and their highest point is marked on most maps as Mathews Peak. The local Samburu name for this highest peak is Ol Doinyo Lenkiyio, usually pronounced 'Lengiyo'.

Many of the other mountains in this region have more than one name: Lololokwe is sometimes written Ololokwe or Lolokwe, and is also called Ol Doinyo Sabachi; Warges is also written Uaraguess (closer to its general pronounciation), and referred to by some local Samburu as Sabachi or Ol Doinyo Wamba.

Although the surrounding plains are dry and dotted with tough thorn trees, the higher areas of the Lenkiyio Hills are covered in lush forest of fig and podocarpus trees. Cycads, one of the oldest plant species on earth, also grow here.

This forest is inhabited by numerous species of wild animal, including elephant, buffalo, leopard, waterbuck, forest hog and the occasional lion or rhino, who have climbed to the higher ground away from the plains which are heavily grazed by domestic animals. The forest is also home to over one hundred species of bird and a large colourful selection of butterflies.

The area around the Lenkiyio/Mathews Range is very remote and away from the usual tourist circuits. There are several places around the hills where walking and camping is possible but, due to the nature of the terrain and the proximity of animals unused to human presence, these are only suitable for the experienced.

An ideal base, however, for exploring the central part of the Lenkiyio/Mathews Range is the Ngeng Valley, which has a tented lodge, called Kitich Camp, and a public campsite. This point is relatively easy to reach and offers several excellent walks. Guides and guards can be arranged and vehicles left safely.

Best time to visit

The rainy season is shorter in the north of Kenya than in the south, but its effects on travel are likely to be just as serious. During the rainy months of March-April and October-November, driving conditions on dirt roads are

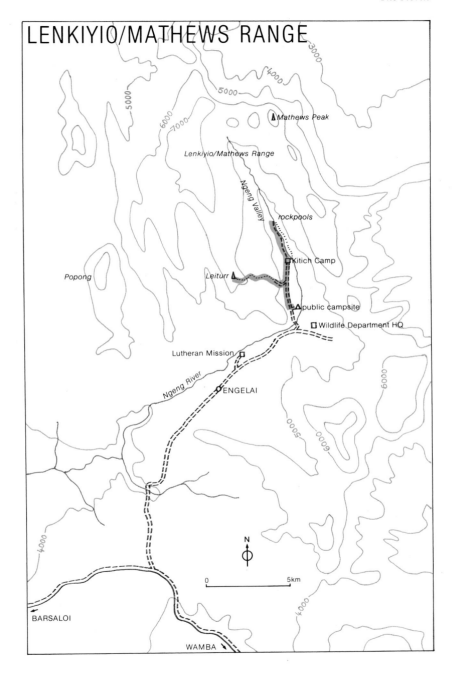

difficult or even dangerous. River beds, known as luggas, which are dry most of the year become swollen by flood water and are impossible for even powerful vehicles to cross. Bridges are frequently washed away effectively closing a road for many months at a time. The best time to visit is in the dry seasons, December-February and May-September, but weather patterns are increasingly unpredictable so drivers aiming for Kitich Camp should check that the roads are passable with the local police, or with the camp through their Nairobi agent.

Special conditions
Kitich Camp hold a lease on an area of land around the camp which is reserved for the sole use of their guests. Walkers using the public campsites may be asked not to pass through this area.

Warning
The Ngeng Valley is densely vegetated and inhabited by several species of potentially dangerous animals. Walkers should be accompanied by a guide at all times.

Maps
The Lenkiyio/Mathews Range is covered by the SK series Y503 1:250M sheet NA-37-9 (Maralal). The whole range is also covered by the SK series Y731 1:50M sheets 79/1, 79/2, 79/3 and 79/4. The Ngeng Valley and the area around Kitich Camp (including Leiturr) is covered by sheet 79/4. Mathews Peak is on sheet 79/2, although 79/1 is also useful as it shows part of the approach route. Older indices show that the Lenkiyio/Mathews Range is also covered by SK series Y633 1:100M sheet 79.

Approach
The Lenkiyio/Mathews Range lies about 160km directly to the north of Mount Kenya, about 430km by road from Nairobi. The best way for drivers from Nairobi is via Thika, Karatina, Nanyuki and Isiolo (270km). The tar stops at Isiolo and this is the last place where petrol is available.

From Isiolo follow the main road north towards Marsabit, Moyale and the Ethiopian border. The road is graded but rough. Pass the entrances to Samburu and Buffalo Springs National Reserves and through the small centre of Archer's Post. Continue for 22km beyond Archer's Post to turn left (before the large, steep-sided, orange block of Lololokwe) onto a good dirt road, signposted Wamba. Follow this dirt road for 36km to a fork. Take the right branch to cross a large lugga by a concrete bridge, then after a further 10km fork right (signposted Wamba), and left after 0.5km (signposted Barsaloi). (The road to the right at this junction leads to Wamba, reached after 5km.)

Follow the dirt road towards Barsaloi for 15km to a fork; take the right branch (marked by two yellow stones) and follow the track for 17km to reach the small centre of Engelai. This track is generally in good condition but it does cross a number of deep sandy luggas and four-wheel drive is essential. From Engelai the track drops into a valley and runs to the right (south-east) of the Ngeng River crossing several more luggas. Near the Lutheran Mission, 2km beyond Engelai, fork right, then 7km from Engelai fork left (the right fork leads to the Wildlife Department H.Q.) to cross the river by a deep ford. Continue on the track for 5km to reach Kitich Camp. (1.5km from the ford another small track on the right leads down to the public campsite.)

From Isiolo to Kitich Camp is 155km, so for a return trip vehicles should have a range of at least 350km. Much of the approach is on dirt road which will increase the petrol consumption considerably.

Public transport is available only as far as Wamba. Beyond here traffic on the roads is extemely light.

Accommodation
Kitich Camp is a tented lodge built in the style of a traditional hunting camp with a group of large safari tents (each with its own shower and toilet) overlooking a bend in the river. The camp has a bar and restaurant serving excellent food, all cooked over wood fires. Animals such as water-buck, warthog and buffalo come to drink on the opposite bank and spotlights have been arranged so that leopards, hyena and the rare honey-badger can be viewed at night.

Various walks are arranged by Kitich Camp in the area around the valley. These range from gentle evening strolls along the river to look at flowers and birds, through longer walks in the morning or afternoon along forest trails to visit deep rock-pools ideal for swimming or picnics, to long full-day hikes up to the various rocky summits above the valley. Experienced Samburu guides accompany walkers and, on certain trips, armed rangers from the Wildlife Department are also provided.

A double tent at Kitich Camp costs 4500/- (fb, 1990). Bookings are recommended. Reservations and further details from Let's Go Travel, Nairobi.

The public campsite is about 3.5km lower down the valley from Kitich Camp. The site belongs to Samburu County Council and the camping fees are collected for the council by Kitich Camp. Askaris are provided during the day, to guard vehicles and tents while campers are out walking, and during the night, to maintain a fire and prevent unwanted visits from nocturnal animals. Guides for walks are provided by Kitich Camp for an extra charge.

Although not essential, bookings for the public campsite are preferred as this allows guides and askaris to be arranged. Reservations and further details from Let's Go Travel, Nairobi.

Walking in the Ngeng Valley
Guides are essential for walks in this area so detailed route descriptions are unnecessary. As an introduction the following walks are briefly described:

Kitich Camp to the Rock Pools
2 - 3 hours

This is a pleasant walk up the Ngeng Valley upstream from Kitich Camp through dense forest, interspersed with patches of open grassland, on clear paths. The path on the west bank has been cleared in sections and, to avoid backtracking, another less well-defined path can be followed back to the camp down the east bank. The pools make an excellent half-way resting place and at least another hour should be added to the walking time to allow for swimming and sunbathing on the smooth rocks beside the river.

To Leiturr Summit
4 - 5 hours

Leiturr is one of a group of rocky summits at the southern end of the main south-west spur which forms the western side of the Ngeng Valley. From a point on the drivable track, about half-way between Kitich Camp and the public campsite a faint, but still drivable, track leads in an easterly direction up towards the crest of the spur. A vehicle could follow this track for about 1km until it peters out at a vague roadhead. There is no single well-defined footpath but a series of trails, used by the Samburu to bring cattle up to the higher slopes for grazing, lead towards the top.

The trails pass through dense bush on the lower slopes but this gives way to lighter cover and frequent grassy clearings as height is gained. At the crest of the spur it is not clear which is the actual highest point; some maps mark Leiturr as a particular summit although the local Samburu refer to the whole group of peaks as Leiturr. From the summit the lower section of the Ngeng Valley can be seen below and to the east. To the south-west the flat red plains, dotted with acacia and scrub, stretch towards Marti Seramit, the long flat-topped ridge visible in the distance. The road from Wamba towards Maralal passes through the obvious semi-circular gap in this ridge

From the drivable track to the high peaks of Leiturr is $1^1/_2$ - 2 hours (2 - $2^1/_2$ hours from Kitich Camp or the public site). Allow 1 - $1^1/_2$ hours ($1^1/_2$ - 2 hours) for the return walk.

Maralal

Maralal is a large town on the main road from Nairobi to the east shore of Lake Turkana, roughly half-way between the Central Highlands and the lake. The town is a major trading centre, the district administrative headquarters and the unofficial capital of the Samburu 'nation'.

To the north of Maralal lies a highland region which is unnamed on most maps, although Poror (2583m/8,473ft), the highest point and at the centre of the region, is usually marked. This region is known as the

Cycad in Kitich Valley   *Candelabra near Maralal*

Leroghi Hills, although this can cause confusion with the Leroghi Forest which also includes the Karisia Hills, to the west of Maralal. Paths in this area are indistinct (where they exist at all) and the steep, densely forested, valleys are home to various species of wild animal, including elephant, buffalo, hyena and lion, and so the region cannot be recommended for walkers or campers unless very experienced.

Maralal town, however, makes an ideal base from which to explore the area just to the south of the Leroghi Hills. Here conditions are pleasant and walkers can cross undulating country, passing through lightly wooded areas, where Samburu people live in scattered manyattas and herdsmen graze their cattle. Away from the grassland, walkers with an experienced guide can reach the higher forested areas to visit rocky outcrops with impressive views across the surrounding hills and the plains beyond.

Approach routes are straightforward and Maralal has a lodge, a hostel and a campsite where guides can be arranged and vehicles safely left.

Best time to visit
Maralal can be reached at any time of the year, except when flash floods during the rainy season close the road temporarily, but it is best to visit during dry periods, December-February and June-September, when conditions are easier for walking. Weather patterns are unpredictable, however, and walkers intending to visit the Maralal area can enquire about local conditions at the Nairobi offices of the lodge and hostel.

171

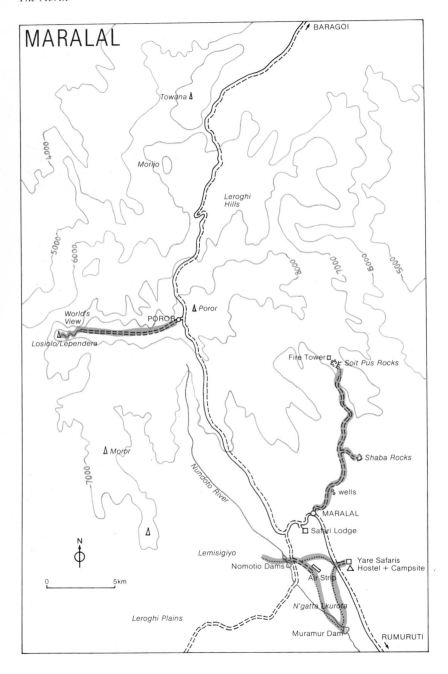

MARALAL

Warning
The area around Maralal has been gazetted as a national sanctuary, where wildlife is protected. Along the road, and around the lodge and hostel, walkers may see zebra and gazelle, but further away from human habitation larger animals, such as lion, leopard and buffalo may be encountered. Visitors are recommended not to walk without an experienced local guide.

Approach
Maralal lies about 250km directly to the north of Nairobi. The best approach route for drivers is via Naivasha, Gilgil, Nyahururu and Rumuruti; 320km by road. The roads are tarred to Rumuruti, but the graded road beyond is regularly maintained and generally in good condition. High grade petrol is not available beyond Nyahururu, although in Maralal diesel and low-grade fuel can be bought.

One bus and at least one matatu runs each way every day between Nyahururu and Maralal, and more regularly between Nyahururu and Nakuru, Nyeri or Nairobi. Traffic is light on the Nyahururu - Maralal road so hitching a ride requires patience.

The hostel and campsite in Maralal operate a transfer bus service from Nairobi (details below).

Accommodation
Maralal has two places to stay which make suitable bases for walking in the area.

Maralal Safari Lodge is about 3km outside the town, clearly signposted, just off the main dirt road to Baragoi and the north. Guests at the lodge stay in roomy self-contained chalets built of local cedar, each with a low balcony overlooking a waterhole where various animals, including zebra, gazelle and monkey, come to drink, (d 2030/- hb, 2119/- fb, 1990). Short walks are organized each morning and evening; an experienced guide leads visitors through the lightly forested area around the lodge to view the animals and birds. Longer walks through the forest or to visit a nearby manyatta can also be arranged. A vehicle and driver can also be hired by prior arrangement. For enquiries and reservations contact Thorn Tree Safaris, P.O. Box 42475, Kaunda Street, Nairobi, Tel 25641, 28981, 25941.

Yare Safaris Hostel and Campsite is about 4km south of Maralal, on the right (east) side of the road coming in from Rumuruti. Guests can choose between comfortable bandas, set in the hostel grounds but with views over the surrounding countryside (d 470/- 1990), or dormitory accommodation inside the hostel (70/-). The hostel has a lounge and common room, and a restaurant which is open all day. The grassy campsite is secure with a clean water supply, showers and toilets (40/-).

The hostel is officially recognized by the Kenyan Youth Hostels Association, part of the International Youth Hostel Federation, and discounts on camping and dormitory accommodation are given to YHA members. Organized walking safaris, inclusive of all food and accommodation, are arranged (600/- per day), or visitors may hire a guide (150/- per day) and choose a destination to suit their own interest and abilities. Yare Safaris employ local Samburu morans as guides; all speak English and are very knowledgeable about the surrounding area, its wildlife and people. The senior guide is Idi Lewarani, who is cheerful, knowledgeable and highly recommended.

Yare Safaris also organize a selection of safaris and expeditions from Nairobi and Maralal to places further afield using four-wheel drive trucks or camels. They are also the only company running overland tours to visit the gorillas in Zaire. A special transfer service (free for YHA members) runs between Nairobi and the Maralal hostel. YHA members also qualify for discounts on all tours organized by Yare Safaris. For reservations and enquiries contact Yare Safaris Adventure Travel Centre , 1st floor, Union Towers, Corner Moi Ave/Mama Ngina St, PO Box 63006, Nairobi, Tel 725610, 725618.

Maps
The Series Y503 1:250M sheet NA-37-9 (Maralal) covers the area around Maralal and the Lenkiyio/Mathews Range. The area around Maralal is also shown on Series Y731 1:50M sheet 78/3.

Walking in the Maralal area
Guides are required for all but the shortest routes covered in this section, so detailed route descriptions are unnnecessary. The following destinations are recommended and provide a range of walks varying in distance and seriousness.

Yare Safaris Hostel to Maralal Town
1 - 2 hours

This is a pleasant short walk which can be done with or without a guide, depending on the route taken. From the hostel, turn immediately right at the main gate to follow a small path past the staff quarters on the right, then down through a clump of trees in a hollow to join a wide path that runs parallel with the main road into Maralal town. The path crosses a dirt road at right angles after 0.5km; continue straight on through lightly wooded grassland, past some manyattas. After 3km (45 minutes - 1 hour) the path tops a rise and Maralal town is clearly visible and reached after a further 1km.

It is also possible to walk from the hostel to the town via the small, lightly wooded, hills that lie to the right (east) of the main road and path described above. There are many paths in this area, and it is not possible to describe a single route, however the walk into Maralal via the hills is recommended as it provides good views of the surrounding area. From the hills it is possible to see Maralal and the hostel so walkers are unlikely to get lost, but first-time visitors may prefer to take a guide.

Maralal town consists mainly of two wide dusty streets, lined with wooden-fronted shops, and a large market, but it is nonetheless an interesting place to wander around. Local Samburu from the plains and hills come into town to buy or sell wares or just catch up on the news. Fully decorated morans strut along the middle of the streets while old *mzees* (old men) wrapped in blankets huddle together on corners. Women and young girls congregate outside the shops and sit on the wide verandas. The shops tend to be run by Kikuyu and Somali people, and Maralal also has a large Turkana community.

Visitors can visit the market, where a few stalls sell traditional Samburu or Turkana artefacts, or Kenyatta House, where Jomo Kenyatta, then the leader of Kenya's independence movement, was imprisoned by the colonial authorities in 1961. The house is now a national monument and is signposted up the hill to the north of the main dirt road between Maralal town and the Safari Lodge. It is almost empty, and not particularly interesting inside, but from the small veranda visitors can look down over Maralal town and out to the hills and plains beyond. On a clear day Mount Kenya is visible on the distant horizon. When Kenyatta was imprisoned here he would apparently spend many hours of contemplation on this veranda, facing Mount Kenya.

Yare Safaris Hostel to Lemisigiyo and the Nundoto Dams
5 - 6 hours

The area to the south-west of Maralal is known as N'gatta Lkuroto (marked on the SK map as Ongatta Olkuroto). Through this area cuts the River Nundoto, one of many rivers that flow south from the Leroghi Hills. Some of these rivers disappear in the dry season but the Nundoto, although reduced to a narrow muddy stream, continues to flow. The river has been dammed in a number of places to create small lakes (also called 'dams' locally), which provide water for the Samburu cattle and the many birds that congregate here, and these make pleasant destinations for a half-day walk.

Beyond N'gatta Lkuroto is an area called Lemisigiyo. In a small collection of huts here, blacksmiths make tools to sell in the market and spears for the local morans. Walkers can visit a forge and buy crude but interesting souvenirs. (A small Samburu spear takes on more significance if you have seen it actually being made.)

From the hostel three of the main Nundoto dams can be combined in a circular walk which also takes in a visit to the blacksmiths at Lemisigiyo: Hostel to Muramur Dam, 1 hour; Muramur Dam to Nomotio Old Dam, $1^1/_2$ hours; Nomotio Old Dam to Lemisigiyo, 1 hour; return to hostel, via Nomotio New Dam, $1^1/_2$ hours. (Guide recommended.)

Maralal to Soit Pus Rocks and Shaba Rocks

To the north-east of Maralal the land rises towards the Leroghi Hills, and is divided by numerous valleys and ridges formed by the streams running down from the higher ground. The valleys in this area are densely forested but the ridge tops are clear and offer fine open walking with excellent views of the surrounding region. Particularly good viewpoints are the two high rock outcrops of Soit Pus and Shaba.

There seems to be some confusion over the nomenclature of these features. According to local people, the outcrop 5km from Maralal is called Shaba (although this is marked on the SK 250M map as Soit Pus), and the outcrop further to the north, 13km from Maralal is Soit Pus (marked as Lole). The local names are used on the map in this book.

The numerous paths that wind through the forest cannot be described accurately and the one drivable track that does exist is overgrown and badly eroded in places. Also, in these forested areas, an encounter with a wild animal is more likely, so to reach either of these rocks walkers are strongly recommended to take a guide.

Shaba Rocks is a jumble of huge scattered boulders perched high on the steep crest of a ridge. Hyrax bask on the warm stones, and in the valleys below zebra and gazelle graze peacefully. From Maralal town to Shaba Rocks is 7km of open walking. The return journey takes 4 - 6 hours. A number of circular walks with Shaba as the midway point are possible. On the way to Shaba along the track walkers pass the area outside Maralal where the Turkana people live. It is interesting to contrast their round huts and shambas with the traditional Samburu manyattas. About 5km from Maralal this track crosses the bed of an old river and passes a group of Samburu pit-wells. These deep holes have been dug with terraces cut into their sides allowing morans to form a human chain and pass buckets of water from the bottom of the pit to a cattle trough at the top.

Soit Pus Rocks also mark the head of a ridge but are higher than Shaba with steep cliffs on their eastern side. Above the rocks on the ridge itself is a large fire watchtower and from here it is possible to see back to Maralal and, if conditions are clear, across the plains beyond to Mount Kenya on the horizon. To the east, beyond the wide expanse of the Suare Plains, much of the chain of northern ranges can be seen on the horizon, from Warges in the south, through the Lenkiyio/Mathews Range, to the Ndoto Mountains in the north. The wide gap of the Malgis valley can be seen between the ridges of Lenkiyio and the Ndotos. Walkers aiming for Soit Pus can also visit Shaba Rocks and the pit-wells previously mentioned.

From Maralal to Soit Pus Rocks is 18km. The walking conditions are good but only the fittest hikers would be able to cover the return distance in a day. With a car and some intrepid driving it is possible to reach a point about 2km south of Soit Pus and walk the rest of the way. To include more walking, and avoid some of the worst sections of track, a car could

Rohan

CLOTHES FOR THE *ACTIVE* MIND

Rohan was conceived fourteen years ago as the first real alternative to conventional outdoor wear. Since then it has grown to become the definitive (and most respected) clothing system available.

All of our garments must cope beyond question with the extremes of whatever climatic or environmental conditions they are likely to be worn in. That is why our range is based on the "layer" principle of dressing. This allows the basic garments to be used all the year round in most climates, with the addition or omission of other items as required. Because Rohan clothing works like no other, it looks like no other. Our philosophy has always been "Function dictates form." We design primarily with performance in mind, thereby setting Rohan apart.

BRIGHTON, 6 Nile Pavilion, Nile St. Tel: 0273 822652
BRISTOL, 10 Welshback, Tel: 0272 292594
CHICHESTER, 6 Priory Lanes Arcade, Northgate, Tel: 0243 787214
COVENT GARDEN, 10 Henrietta St, Covent Garden, Tel: 01-831 1059
EDINBURGH, 86 George St, Edinburgh, Tel: 031-225 4876
GLASGOW, 133 Buchanan St, Glasgow, Tel: 041-204 0775
HALE, 197 Ashley Road, Hale, Nr. Altrincham, Tel: 061-928 9511
KENSINGTON, 5 Kensington High St, Tel: 071-938

LONG PRESTON, Main St, Long Preston, Tel: 07294 611
MILTON KEYNES, 1-3 Knebworth Gate, Giffard Park, Tel: 0908 615407
NEWCASTLE, 17 Eldon Garden, Eldon Sq. Tel: 091-261 0033
STRATFORD, 23-24 Wood St, Stratford-upon-Avon, Tel: 0789 414498
SUTTON COLDFIELD, 188-189 Gracechurch Centre, Tel: 021-355 7006
YORK, 24 Stonegate, York, Tel: 0904 651606.

ROHAN FRANCHISE SHOPS
AMBLESIDE, Compston Rd, Tel: 05394 32946
KESWICK, 19 Lake Road, Tel: 07687 74963
LYTHAM ST. ANNES, 37 Wood St, St. Annes on Sea, Tel: 0253 713737

ROHAN DESIGNS PLC — 30 Maryland Road, Tongwell, Milton Keynes, Bucks, MK15 8HN. Tel: 0908 618888.

be left at a manyatta (your guide will help), or an askari could be arranged at the lodge or hostel to ride in your car and guard it while you are walking.

Idi, the senior guide at Yare Safaris Hostel, can arrange a two-day walk to Soit Pus Rocks, which includes a night camping near the watchtower. Walkers should be self-contained. Water must also be carried as there is none at the rocks. Food can be bought in Maralal. Firewood should be collected on the way as it gets cold at night. (The fire will also serve as a warning to the wild animals in the area that humans are nearby.) Porters, or a second guide, to carry extra equipment or supplies, can also be arranged, with prior notice and for an extra fee.

Losiolo and World's View

The highest point of the Leroghi Hills is Poror (2583m/8,473ft), 25km by road north of Maralal, near the small centre of the same name, about 0.5km and less than ten minutes' walk from the main dirt road. On top of the peak is a tall radio mast. As the road tops this summit area the land drops away to the north and west towards the Rift Valley. The Rift escarpment is at its steepest, and the views at their most spectacular, at a point 10km to the west of Poror called Losiolo where the land drops suddenly, over 1000m, down to the Rift Valley floor.

On some maps Losiolo is indicated as a specific peak, but the local people refer to this entire section of the escarpment as Losiolo and each hill or spur has its individual name. The highest point is called Lependera.

It is possible to drive from Maralal, via Poror, to the edge of the escarpment some 2km to the north of Lependera. This place is called Malaso locally, although it is more popularly known as World's View, and the views from here are excellent. Particularly dramatic is the early morning when the warm air rising causes great clouds of mist to rush, almost vertically, up the escarpment wall.

The drivable track ends at World's View, from where the higher peak of Lependera can be seen, beyond another large spur, to the left (south). A path leads towards it, crossing a grassy area, and keeping the escarpment edge to the right, before dropping and climbing through a thickly vegetated valley. Another grassy area is crossed and a second vegetated valley reached. The spur between these two valleys is called Olgerigero. Beyond the second valley another grassy area slopes up to the summit of Lependera (1 - $1^1/_2$ hours from World's View).

The views from this point are even more spectacular than at World's View. To the north Lake Turkana is occasionally visible, and to the north-east it is possible to see across the Leroghi Hills to the Ndoto Mountains. To the south-west Lake Baringo can be glimpsed and, on the horizon slightly to the right (north-west) of the lake, the Cherangani Hills mark the other side of the Rift Valley.

Walkers without a car can still reach Lependera. Matatus run about five times per day between Maralal and Barsaloi via Poror, from where it is possible to walk across the narrow plateau of farmland to World's View (10km, 2 - 3 hours). If time allows, walkers can reach Lependera (by following the directions above) then return to Poror to catch the matatu back to Maralal.

To make a visit to Losiolo easier, a car and driver can be hired through Maralal Safari Lodge. Alternatively, one of the guides from Yare Safaris Hostel will accompany you on the matatu and then walk with you to World's View or the summit of Lependera.

Updates

Readers using this guidebook should note that in Africa changes happen regularly and without warning, and should be prepared for increased prices, re-built roads, discontinued bus routes, damaged bridges, closed footpaths, missing signposts, renamed hotels and new regulations. Readers noting errors or omissions, or with comments and suggestions to make, are invited to write to the publishers at 17-18 Angel Gate, City Road, London EC1V 2PT.

Index of major place names

Page numbers refer to the main references to each place.